#63
A Journey Through Sacred Memories

Rizwan Hussain

I dedicate this book to my father, my mother, my wife,
and my sons—Zayn, Raiyyan (late), and Deen.
You are the anchors of my life and the reason I strive
to be better. This book is as much for you as it is for its readers—
a testament to faith, family, and the enduring love that binds us all.

Contents

Foreword (Sheikh Abdur Rahman Madani) 7

Foreword (Muhammad Asadullah, PhD) 9

Introduction 11

Chapter 1: My First Dua at Sighting the Ka'bah 15

Chapter 2: 5 Years Later:A New Journey to Makkah and Madinah 25

Chapter 3: Umrah with my Late Father 33

Chapter 4: The Transformative First Hajj, 2005 41

Chapter 5: The Working Hajj 65

Chapter 6: Makkah Twin Peaks 87

Chapter 7: Footsteps of the Prophet PBUH 93

Chapter 8: The Umrah of Mourning & Glad Tidings 115

Chapter 9: Umrah Guide 121

Chapter 10: The Basics of Umrah 133

Acknowledgements 141

Foreword

أحمد الله حمد الشاكرين وأصلي وأسلم علي النبي الأمين وعلى آله الطيبين الطاهرين وصحبه أجمعين وبعد!

Allah SWT has selected Makkah and Madinah to spread His chosen religion 'Islam'. He SWT has given these two holy lands a magnetic power to attract people from around the world. A Muslim's most important desire of this life would be visiting Makkah and Madinah and performing Hajj and Umrah. Every visitor must have a story tell, a memory to remember, a change in life to bring about, a motivation to come back with; **but some stories are exceptional, some memories are life changing.**

Barrister Rizwan Hussain's "#63 A Journey Through Sacred Memories" is a real-life changing experience. It's very easy to read, quick to take lesson and long lasting in motivation.

It's not a direct Hajj or Umrah Guide but it is more than a guide as it will -in sha Allah- change lives of many generations to come. I feel very humbled and privileged that I was involved in some of his journeys to share my little knowledge that Allah SWT has bestowed upon me with His infinite mercy. I hope and pray that this book will be a strong source of inspiration for many people around the world. May Allah SWT accept this book as a Sadaqah Jariyah for the author and for all of us. Ameen.

رَبَّنَا تَقَبَّلْ مِنَّاۖ إِنَّكَ أَنتَ السَّمِيعُ الْعَلِيمُ وَتُبْ عَلَيْنَاۖ إِنَّكَ أَنتَ التَّوَّابُ الرَّحِيمُ

Sheikh Abdur Rahman Madani

Foreword

The act of Hajj and Umrah has long held a unique place in the hearts of the Muslims. It is a journey not just of the body but of the soul—a voyage of self-discovery, surrender, and connection to the divine. In A Journey Through Sacred Memories, Barrister Rizwan Hussain captures the essence of such a pilgrimage, one that transcends mere physical travel to reflect on the profound transformations of the heart and soul.

This book is a testament to Barrister Rizwan's remarkable devotion, encapsulating his 63 journeys to Makkah and Madinah over nearly three decades. Being invited as the guest of Ar-Rahman on 63 occasions is an extraordinary blessing and a rare honour. Rarely does a narrative so seamlessly blend personal reflection, communal experiences, and profound spiritual awakening. Each chapter of this book offers a window into Barrister Rizwan's deeply personal encounters with the sacred, making it as much a guide to the holy cities as it is a meditation on faith and purpose.

Barrister Rizwan's eloquence and humility resonate throughout his storytelling. His reflections remind us that sacred experiences are not confined to ritual but are found in every step of the journey, from the quiet Duaas at the Ka'bah to the bustling streets of Makkah and the serene embrace of Madinah. Through his vivid descriptions, readers are transported to these holy places, feeling the weight of history and the closeness of divine presence.

This work also speaks to Barrister Rizwan's life beyond his pilgrimages. As a barrister, broadcaster, and philanthropist, his contributions to community upliftment are profound. Yet it is in these journeys, in the simplicity of faith, humility and surrender, that he finds his truest anchor. By sharing his story, he offers not only inspiration but also guidance for those yearning to deepen their own connection to the divine.

#63 is more than a collection of memories; it is an invitation to reflect on the sacredness of our own journeys, no matter where they may lead. This book speaks to seekers, pilgrims, and anyone yearning to find solace and meaning in the rhythms of devotion and faith.

As you turn these pages, may you find yourself inspired to seek, to reflect, and, like Barrister Rizwan, to surrender fully to the call of Allah Subhanahu Wa Ta'ala.

Muhammad Asadullah, PhD

Associate Professor,
Department of Justice Studies
University of Regina, Regina, SK, Canada

Introduction

This book, titled simply #63, marks a personal milestone—a journey through memories spanning 63 visits to Makkah and Madinah. Each visit isn't just a trip; it's a moment suspended in time, a thread in the fabric of nearly three decades, woven with hope, solace, and a search for deeper connection. This October, I was blessed—Alhamdulillah—to complete my 63rd visit. Every journey, every step in those holy lands, has left an imprint on my soul, shaping who I am today. It's been 28 years of going back, and each time, I come away changed.

Why write this? Why share these experiences now? Because there's something profound about being called, time and again, to the same sacred place. I look back on these years and realise that each journey was more than an act of worship; it was a mirror showing me my true self. Through the highs and lows, Makkah has been my constant, my haven, my place of solace. And I want others to feel this, to understand that these journeys aren't just physical—they're journeys of the heart and soul.

Of the 63 visits, 11 were for Hajj. Each one of those was special in its own way. But the majority were Umrah trips, often as a guide leading groups. I started back in 2006, driven by a simple desire to share the beauty of this journey with others. I remember talking with a close friend after my 10th visit, saying, "Maybe I should start sharing what I've experienced." Little did I know that this calling would lead me back, over and over again, each time a different story, each time a new lesson.

Many of these journeys were deeply personal. Some were made alone, while others were with family, siblings, or, more recently, my own children. Each trip had its own unique purpose, a way of steering my life, often when I needed it most. Makkah became my anchor, the place where I found clarity in the midst of chaos, where I felt truly seen and understood.

Life, as we know, is unpredictable. We're tossed between moments of joy and hardship. For me, returning to Makkah has always felt like a lifeline, a reminder that no matter what life throws my way, Allah has called me to be His guest. And that knowledge, that invitation, has been my source of hope. It's as if He's saying, "No matter where you are or what you're going through, I am here, and you are welcome."

Some Umrahs stand out vividly in my memory; others blur together, marked simply by the companions who joined me. Yet there are always certain moments that stay with me, unforgettable and precious. It's those moments that I hope to share here, those small encounters that left lasting marks.

This book has two purposes. First, it's a glimpse into the experiences of a traveller blessed with the privilege of frequent visits—sharing the good, the challenging, and the deeply moving. Second, it's about the journey of learning, the ways these visits have transformed me, especially under the guidance of incredible scholars. They've influenced not only how I see the world but also how I lead and support others on their own journeys.

Perhaps another reason to call this book #63 is because our beloved Prophet (PBUH) lived to that age. For me, this number holds not only the significance of my own journey but also a connection to his life—a reminder that even in the impermanence of life, there is a call to purpose, to growth, and to faith. Each visit, like each year of his life, has been a step toward understanding, a reminder of the beauty and depth of faith.

So, Bismillah. With this introduction, I pray that #63 becomes more than just words on a page. I hope it inspires, moves, and, most importantly, draws readers closer to Makkah and Madinah. This is my story, my soul's journey, and I hope it ignites a spark in those who read it—a yearning to visit, to connect, and to keep returning, Insha'Allah.

Rizwan Hussain

CHAPTER 1

My First Dua at Sighting the Ka'bah

There's no place better to start this journey than at the very beginning—the first time I was blessed to set eyes upon the Kaaba. It feels like a lifetime ago, back in 1996. I was 22, just out of my studies in London, having completed my Bar exams. I was carrying the weight of my father's dream on my shoulders; he had longed to see me become a barrister, a title that he felt would bring respect and honour to our family. I was striving to make that dream a reality, yet something inside was searching for more, for a meaning beyond professional success.

Each day, I walked the familiar streets of East London, heading toward Brick Lane to shadow a senior barrister. Along the way, I passed a small travel agency called TravelLink. Sami Sanaullah, the brother who ran it, has now been a part of my life for many years. Back then, however, I hardly knew him. Every time I passed that agency, I felt an inexplicable pull, a quiet whisper from Allah Himself. It was as though my soul sensed a need I hadn't yet understood—a desire for peace, for clarity, for a connection that could anchor me. The weight of exams, uncertainty about the future, and a longing for deeper purpose grew with each day. One day, that pull became impossible to ignore.

Without fully knowing why, I stepped into the agency and asked about Umrah. In 1996, the concept of Umrah wasn't common in our community; people generally saved for Hajj, and it was rare for someone my age to venture on such a journey alone. Sami must have sensed the mixture of uncertainty and hope in my voice, for he simply nodded and said I could buy a ticket to Jeddah. No package, no guide—just a ticket to somewhere unknown. I bought it right then, called my father, and told him I was going to perform Umrah in the last ten days of Ramadan. I still remember the softness in his voice when he said, "If you're going to Makkah, you should visit a family from our neighbouring village in Bangladesh; they run a small house for pilgrims."

Preparing for this journey felt both exhilarating and daunting. Ihram garments were not readily available, so I bought two pieces of pure cotton of equal length and carefully packed them. With a small bag containing £120 and not much else, I headed to the airport. Boarding the Saudi Airlines flight felt like stepping into another realm. I was no longer just a young man chasing a career; I was a pilgrim, answering a call that seemed as ancient as time itself.

Landing in Jeddah was a sensory awakening—the heat, the hum of Arabic, the unfamiliar chaos. It felt foreign and yet, in some indescribable way, familiar, as though I'd been meant to be there all along. Outside the airport, men called out, "Haram, haram!" offering rides. Soon, I found myself on the back of an open-air pickup truck with other pilgrims, all dressed in white, their faces reflecting the same mix of awe and anticipation I felt. The journey to Makkah felt sacred, each mile bringing me closer to a place I had longed for without even realizing it.

As we entered Makkah, my heart raced. This was the city of the Prophet, the city my father had spoken of with reverence. Following his directions, I found the house of a brother named Hifzur Rahman, who ran a lodging called Dar Abu Mansoor. Tucked behind heavy wooden doors, down narrow streets, the house held an air of timelessness. The Rahman family welcomed me with open arms, as if I were one of their own, offering me food, shelter, and their precious time. Brother Hifzur's kindness left an indelible mark on me. Years later, he would move to London and establish Labbayk Travels, one of the largest Umrah and Hajj providers, but in those early days, his hospitality meant the world to me.

That evening, his brother, a soft-spoken Mawlana, pulled me aside. With a gentle intensity, he said, "Tomorrow, after Fajr, I'll take you to perform Umrah. When you see the Kaaba for the first time, make a dua from your heart because whatever you ask, Allah will answer." His words settled over me like a blessing, igniting a spark of hope I hadn't felt in a long time. That night, I sat on the floor, pen in hand, carefully crafting a list of prayers, each word chosen as if Allah Himself would read it. I wanted to leave nothing unsaid.

The next morning, as we walked toward the Haram, my heart pounded with anticipation. The Mawlana advised me to keep my eyes down, to hold back my gaze until I was directly before the Kaaba. I tucked my list into my Ihram and focused on each step, feeling the sacredness of the moment thick in the air, as if every breath was infused with barakah.

And then, there it was—the Kaaba. I reached for my list, but it was gone. In the stillness of that moment, I lifted my gaze and saw the Kaaba for the very first time. I was breathless, struck silent, utterly overwhelmed. Every thought, every prayer I had prepared, faded away. I was standing before Allah's House, and all I could do was surrender.

One prayer escaped my lips, unplanned and raw: "Ya Allah, You have brought me here to Your House. Bring me back here, again and again, as many times as You will." It wasn't on my list, yet it felt like the only dua that mattered. Stripped of all pretence, my heart laid bare, I stood in a purity of intention I hadn't known before. That prayer, spoken from the depths of my soul, became the anchor of my life, drawing me back to Makkah 63 times over the years.

As I began my tawaf, circling the Kaaba, I felt an indescribable peace, as though every burden I carried was being lifted with each step. The Black Stone was within reach, and I felt a closeness to Allah that words could never capture. Over those ten days, I performed Umrah after Umrah, each one an offering for my family, pouring my heart into every act of worship.

The Makkah of 1996 was different from today. It had a humbling simplicity that allowed pilgrims to experience it in a pure, undistracted way. The Haram was surrounded by narrow streets that wound around humble shops and modest homes. High-rise hotels were yet to dominate the skyline, and a feeling of intimacy permeated the city. Walking through Makkah, I felt as though I was part of a centuries-old tradition, a long line of believers who had made the

same journey, who had walked these streets with the same awe and reverence.

The streets outside the Haram were lively, filled with merchants selling prayer beads, Zamzam water, dates, and other simple tokens of faith. Each vendor called out in Arabic, smiling and gesturing with open hands, their hospitality unmistakable. The air was thick with the scent of oud, the warmth of freshly baked flatbread, and the whispers of pilgrims from all corners of the world. In those narrow alleys, I felt a strong sense of community—a shared purpose that transcended language and nationality.

Makkah's nights in 1996 were equally enchanting. Without the heavy glow of neon lights and commercial billboards, the city seemed to rest under a blanket of stars. The Haram itself, though smaller than today, glowed with an ethereal light, its marble floors illuminated by gentle lamps. Pilgrims gathered in the cool night air, their voices blending in whispered prayers that rose like a soft hum. It was a place and time where faith felt tangible, woven into the very fabric of the city.

I stayed in Makkah until a day after Eid ul-Fitr, blessed to perform the Eid prayer with the Kaaba before me. The joy and unity I felt standing with thousands of other believers was indescribable, a celebration of faith and gratitude that left me with a profound sense of purpose. The air was alive with takbeer, the sound of voices lifting in praise and thanks, filling the Haram with a vibration that seemed to reach the heavens.

As we stood in prayer, shoulder to shoulder, I felt the depth of the moment. Each person there, like me, had their own journey, their own hopes, their own prayers. Yet, in that moment, we were one, united by faith and the shared gratitude of having been called to this sacred place. The sight of the Kaaba, standing resolute and timeless, gave me a sense of peace I had never felt before. This was more than a city—it was a place of pure devotion, where the soul felt stripped of worldly concerns, open and vulnerable before Allah.

After Makkah, I made my way to Madinah. The transition between these two cities is profound: where Makkah is intense and powerful, Madinah is gentle, like a mother's embrace. As I entered the city, I felt an immediate sense of calm. The streets of Madinah had a softness to them, and the people carried a warmth that mirrored the Prophet's spirit. This was the city that had welcomed him, that had been the centre of his life and mission.

Al-Masjid an-Nabawi, with its distinctive green dome, was a place of peace and light. The mosque was smaller than it is today, and at night, it seemed to glow softly, as though illuminated from within. I spent hours in the Rawdah, the area the Prophet described as a "Garden of Paradise." Sitting there, I felt closer to him than I ever had, feeling his presence in the peace that filled the mosque.

In Madinah, the pace of life slowed, and I found myself immersed in quiet reflection. The souks, or markets, were lively yet respectful. Merchants sold dates, traditional sweets, and small gifts, their voices and laughter mingling with the sounds of children playing. Unlike Makkah's bustling streets, Madinah's had a gentleness that seemed to invite contemplation, to welcome the weary pilgrim and offer rest.

One day, as I sat in the courtyard, a group of young children approached me, their faces bright with smiles. They tugged at my clothes, giggling and inviting me to break the fast with them and their families. Their kindness touched me deeply, a reminder that this city's spirit was not just in its history but in its people, who embodied the teachings of the Prophet (PBUH) in every gesture.

Each of my 63 visits has added another chapter to this ongoing story. With every return, I find new lessons, new perspectives, and new depths of faith. Makkah and Madinah are more than cities; they are places of transformation, where the heart and soul are stripped bare, humbled, and remade. They are cities of the past, yet they offer a glimpse of eternity, of the unwavering connection between the Divine and the human soul.

Returning to the UK felt like emerging from a dream. I left Makkah with a heart full of memories, a soul transformed, and a yearning to return. A few days after I arrived back in London, I went to visit my parents. My father, with his usual quiet pride and respect for sacred places, noticed the cap I was wearing—the same one I had worn throughout my journey. Without a word, he reached over, gently removed it from my head, and held it in his hands for a moment, his fingers reverently brushing over the fabric. Then, in a gesture that took my breath away, he brought the cap to his face and wiped it across his cheeks, as though he were touching the soil of Makkah itself.

"This cap," he murmured, "has touched the soil of Makkah."

That moment stayed with me, growing more precious as the years passed. In his simple act, I saw his love for the holy city and his reverence for Allah. Though he had not walked the journey with me, in that one gesture, he connected to it, sharing in its blessings as only a father could. It was a reminder that our parents carry our journeys in their hearts, that their unseen sacrifices and prayers lift us in ways we may never fully understand.

This memory, like so many others from my numerous journeys to Makkah and Madinah, has shaped my understanding of faith, family, and devotion. It is these memories—moments of awe, gratitude, and deep connection—that I hope to share with you here.

In sharing these experiences, I hope to offer more than memories. #63 is an invitation to experience the beauty, peace, and transformative power of Makkah and Madinah. It is a story of faith, surrender, and discovery—a journey through the heart and soul. May Allah grant each of us the blessing of visiting His House, of walking the paths of His Prophet (PBUH), and of finding in these sacred cities the light that guides us home.

Photo by Ishan on Unsplash (https://unsplash.com/@seefromthesky)

CHAPTER 2

5 Years Later: A New Journey to Makkah and Madinah

Five years had passed since my first unforgettable Umrah. In that time, my life had shifted significantly. I was now working full-time as an immigration lawyer with the Immigration Advisory Service (IAS), a charity dedicated to supporting vulnerable asylum seekers and immigrants. My work had become deeply meaningful but also consuming. Each case I handled seemed to add a weight to my heart, and I felt the need for spiritual rejuvenation—to step away from the demands of life and reconnect with the peace I had once found in Makkah and Madinah. I knew it was time for another journey.

In 2001, the pilgrimage landscape had changed. Umrah packages were now widely available, making the journey more organised than in 1996. Gone were the days of just purchasing a ticket and relying on local hospitality. This time, I arranged a complete Umrah package, including a hotel near the Haram and airport transfers. Although this arrangement offered convenience, I wondered if the structure would alter the raw spiritual intensity I had felt on my first visit.

When I arrived at Jeddah airport, the sights and sounds brought back a flood of memories. The hum of Arabic, the warmth of the evening air, and the sight of pilgrims dressed in white returning home after their own journeys reminded me of my first experience in this sacred land. But this time, instead of a crowded pickup truck, I rode in a proper taxi, driven by a quiet man who skilfully navigated the bustling streets. As we neared Makkah, I felt the familiar excitement of returning, yet I noticed that much had changed. The outskirts of the city were marked by new developments—hotels and shops lined the route, evidence of a growing city adapting to welcome more pilgrims each year.

One of the most noticeable changes was the stairway leading to the Zamzam well, which had been closed off since my last visit. In 1996, I'd descend those steps after tawaf to drink Zamzam directly from its source, feeling deeply connected to the sacred well. It had been a unique experience, to step below the mataaf and sip the water from the well itself, sharing in a tradition that had linked millions before me. Now, that access had been removed, likely for safety reasons, as pilgrims often returned dripping with water, making the mataaf area dangerously slippery. Although I understood the need for these changes, I felt a pang of nostalgia for that intimate connection to the Zamzam well.

The Makkah I now encountered felt much busier. The Haram was encircled by an expanded sea of construction sites and scaffolding, a sign of the mosque's ongoing expansion. Even Misfalah, an area I frequently visited in 1996 for its Bangladeshi restaurants and lively atmosphere, had changed. The once-bustling hub where pilgrims from South Asia gathered for meals and conversation had been transformed. Many of the small eateries and shops were moved farther from the Haram, replaced by larger hotels and an extended piazza designed to accommodate more pilgrims. The road that once led directly to the Haram's entrance had been closed off, replaced by a vast open plaza where pilgrims gathered before prayers, mingling in the bright lights that now illuminated the holy mosque.

Walking through the new piazza, I felt a sense of both awe and nostalgia. I was inspired by the city's effort to accommodate more visitors but felt a twinge of loss for the intimate corners of Makkah that had given it such a unique character. The changes seemed to signal that Makkah was evolving quickly, shedding parts of its old self to make way for an era of growth and modernization. Yet, amid all the transformations, the mountains surrounding Makkah remained. These ancient, silent witnesses to Makkah's history had stood watch over the city for centuries, unmoved by time or the changes below.

Today, the iconic Clock Tower dominates the skyline where a mountain once stood. In 1996, I often climbed that mountain to sit and gaze down at the Kaaba, finding solitude and perspective from above. I remember one particular evening, sitting high above Makkah, absorbing the peace as the sun began to set. The city below sparkled with lights, and the sound of the call to prayer resonated through the air. In that stillness, I met a brother from Afghanistan who had come to perform tawaf before opening his new barbershop near the Haram the next day. As we talked, he told me about the Multazam—a sacred spot on the Kaaba, nestled between the Black Stone and the door, where prayers are known to be answered. He described it with a reverence that spoke to the depth of his own faith, and I felt as though he was sharing a precious secret of Makkah's heart.

With kindness and a spark of excitement, he offered to take me to the Multazam. Together, we descended the mountain and made our way through the bustling crowds around the Haram. He led me to the Kaaba, weaving through worshippers until we stood before the Multazam. There, side by side, we pressed our hands to the Kaaba, lifting our hands in prayer. It was a moment of profound intimacy with Allah, as though every word of our prayers was carried directly to Him. My Afghan brother and I, strangers until that evening, were bound by a shared faith, a shared humility, and a shared hope that our prayers would be answered. That moment before the Multazam has stayed with me ever since, a memory woven into the tapestry of my journeys, reminding me of the beauty of brotherhood and the sanctity of Makkah's hidden blessings.

During this visit in 2001, I tried to recreate those memories. Although the mountain was gone, the essence of that experience remained alive in my heart. I could still feel the solitude and peace that had once accompanied me in that high place. The mountains surrounding Makkah, though changing, were a reminder that, while the city may grow and evolve, the land holds its history and its sanctity, unchanging in its call to believers.

In the hotel near the Haram, I met another young man traveling alone. Seeing him reminded me of my first journey, and without hesitation, I offered him the extra bed in my room. Over the next few days, we shared stories and reflections, bonding over our shared purpose of seeking closeness to Allah. Together, we performed multiple Umrahs, each circuit around the Kaaba reminding me of the essence that remained unchanged despite the city's evolution. The structure of my journey may have changed, but the feeling of stepping into the Haram, of seeing the Kaaba and feeling the vastness of Allah's mercy, remained just as powerful as it had on my first visit. The crowds had grown, and the sounds of construction sometimes filled the air, yet there was a sense of timelessness within the Haram's walls. Each Umrah I performed was an opportunity to reconnect, to let go of the burdens I had accumulated and remind myself of the purpose that had brought me here.

After my time in Makkah, I arranged a taxi to Jeddah airport to catch my flight to Madinah. The anticipation grew as I thought of revisiting the Prophet's city, a place that felt like a balm to the heart. Upon arriving, I found a taxi driver who agreed to take me to my hotel for 15 riyals. But as we navigated the quiet streets, it became clear that finding the hotel was going to be a challenge. The driver circled through unfamiliar alleys, stopping to ask directions from locals, determined to find the place.

Almost two hours passed before we finally arrived. I could see that he had put in a great deal of effort, going above and beyond what he had anticipated for a simple fare. Out of gratitude, I offered him double the agreed amount, explaining that his time and patience deserved more. But he smiled, shaking his head gently. With a humble sincerity that I will never forget, he replied, "This is Madinah—what we agreed is what I will take." His words left a deep impression on me, a reminder that the Prophet's city held not only the sacred mosque but also a spirit of generosity and honour that permeated daily life.

This time, praying in the Rawdah—the blessed area within Al-Masjid an-Nabawi—was not as relaxed as I remembered from my first visit. The peaceful solitude I had once experienced was replaced by a crowd of visitors, each of us hoping for a brief moment in that sacred space. Other worshippers would stand nearby, quietly waiting for their turn, a silent line of anticipation that grew steadily as the hours passed. I could feel their yearning, their reverence, and I knew they, too, had travelled great distances to be here, to offer their prayers in this precious place. Yet, even in the shared crowd, there was an atmosphere of respect and humility as each person waited for their moment to connect with the Prophet's legacy.

As I walked through Madinah, I noticed how much the city itself had changed since my first journey. Many of the old streets and houses that had once lent a distinct charm to the city were gone, replaced by new buildings and roads under construction. The familiar pathways and traditional architecture I remembered had started to disappear, and I realized that Madinah was changing rapidly, just like Makkah.

It was bittersweet to witness this transformation. I felt grateful for the chance to have seen Madinah as it once was, a city of serene streets and intimate neighbourhoods. Yet, I understood that these changes were a sign of progress, a necessary adaptation to accommodate the growing number of visitors. As I walked through the newly paved streets and passed by cranes and scaffolding, I felt a deep appreciation for the timeless essence of Madinah, which continued to endure, even as the outward landscape evolved. The spirit of the Prophet's city remained, a silent, steadfast presence that called us to reflect, to pray, and to remember.

Photo by Haidan on Unsplash (https://unsplash.com/@hydngallery)

CHAPTER 3

Umrah with my Late Father

In 2004, it had been a year since I moved to London, beginning a new chapter as a law lecturer. This move marked a significant transition in my life, bringing new responsibilities and opportunities. Alongside my academic work, I had also ventured into the media world, particularly with Hindi-language channels. It was an exciting time, filled with challenges that pushed me to grow and stretch my abilities in ways I hadn't imagined. Yet, as fulfilling as these new roles were, they also brought with them a certain spiritual void. The fast pace, the constant need to prove myself, and the demands of a new career left me feeling distant from the steady spiritual foundation that had once been central to my life. I missed the quiet, the moments of reflection, and the sense of peace that my faith provided.

When the opportunity arose to return to Makkah for my third Umrah, I seized it without hesitation. I needed this trip—not just as an escape from the pressures of daily life but as a means to reconnect with my faith, to remind myself of what truly mattered. This journey, however, held a special significance beyond my own personal needs: this time, I was taking my father with me. It would be his first return to Makkah since his Hajj in 1983. Over two decades had passed, and Makkah was no longer the same city he had known. While I was eager to revisit the Holy City, my father's anticipation held a different weight, one steeped in memories of a Makkah that had remained preserved in his heart.

As we arrived in Makkah, I watched my father's face, trying to read the emotions that flickered across it. I saw awe, wonder, and a touch of disbelief. The Makkah he remembered was quieter, simpler—a city whose sacred aura was felt in every humble structure and winding street. But now, the towering cranes, expanding skyline, and throngs of pilgrims told a different story. Makkah was transforming, adapting to welcome millions more into its embrace. As we walked through the bustling streets, my father's gaze lingered on the massive new structures that loomed above, and I sensed a hint of sorrow mixed with reverence in his eyes. It was as if he were mourning a Makkah that no longer existed, one that had lived only in his memories.

But then, something shifted. As we approached the Haram, his steps became firmer, and I could sense a renewed energy radiating from him. The old Makkah may have changed, but the heart of Makkah—the Kaaba—stood steadfast, as eternal and unchanging as the faith that binds every pilgrim to it.

There was something profoundly beautiful about performing Umrah with my father, a beauty that went beyond words. It wasn't just the act of worship but the experience of being side by side, our steps falling in sync, our prayers rising together. In that moment, I felt as though we were bridging the space between generations. Each step we took was a reminder of our shared heritage, a journey through time that intertwined his experiences with my own.

As we began our Tawaf, he reached out to me, guiding me with the calm wisdom that only age and experience can bring. Each step around the Kaaba felt as if we were weaving an invisible thread of faith, each prayer stitching us closer together and anchoring us to the divine. With each circuit, my father's stories filled the space between us. His words came quietly, full of a reverent nostalgia, as he described his first Hajj in vivid detail. I could hear the awe in his voice as he recounted laying eyes on the Kaaba for the first time, feeling the overwhelming emotion and humility of being in its presence. He spoke of the simplicity of the rituals back then, the quiet humility that seemed to infuse every moment, every prayer, and every prostration. His words were like a soft echo from the past, bringing to life a Makkah that had been, a place he had carried within him all these years.

As I listened to him, my mind began to drift to something I had read about the angels performing Tawaf above us, in the heavens. I remembered learning about Bait Al Ma'mur, the celestial counterpart to the Kaaba, where the angels themselves circled in worship. It was mentioned in the Qur'an, "And by the Bait Al Ma'mur" (Qur'an 52:4), and the Prophet Muhammad (PBUH) had described it as directly above the Kaaba, where seventy thousand angels enter every day to worship and never return, replaced by others in an unending cycle of devotion (Sahih Bukhari, Hadith 3207). The thought was almost overwhelming—to think that as we circled the Kaaba here on Earth, angels were simultaneously circling Bait Al Ma'mur above, creating a bridge of worship that linked heaven and Earth.

I glanced over at my father as we continued our Tawaf, and a surge of emotion filled my heart. Here we were, two ordinary souls, performing the same act of worship that countless others had performed before us, our humble steps mirrored by the angels in the heavens. It was a reminder that our faith connected us not only to Allah but to the vast cosmos, to the very fabric of creation. In that moment, I felt small yet profoundly significant, like a single thread in the tapestry of the divine. My father's voice brought me back, his gentle reminders of the specific duas to recite, his quiet corrections if I missed a step or faltered in my focus. I realized then that his presence was my anchor, his voice a guide that kept me grounded in each moment.

This realisation brought tears to my eyes, and I looked down, humbled by the weight of what we were part of. Our Tawaf was not merely a ritual but an invitation to join a timeless cycle, a sacred rhythm that had been set in motion since the beginning of creation. The very act of circling the Kaaba was an expression of our submission, a testament to our desire to draw closer to Allah, just as the angels drew close with their endless Tawaf above us. I felt connected not only to my father but to every soul that had ever walked this path, and to the angels who continued their celestial worship in realms we could only imagine.

Over the years, I was blessed to take my father on several more Umrah journeys. Each time, he would look at the Kaaba with the same awe and gratitude, and every time, he would say the same line: "Never did I think I would come back, time and time again." Those words, repeated so often, became etched in my heart—a reflection of his gratitude and wonder at being able to return to the House of Allah, beyond what he had ever dreamed. I watched his connection to Makkah deepen each time, and I knew that for him, each visit was a reminder of Allah's mercy, of the unearned blessings that had allowed him to return again and again.

The last Umrah we performed together was a few years before he passed away, and this time, it was even more special as we were accompanied by other family members. My mother, my sister's husband, and their first child, Zaid, joined us, creating an unforgettable family pilgrimage. Watching my father hold Zaid close—his first grandchild from his eldest daughter—while gazing at the Kaaba, felt like witnessing a full circle of life and faith. I could see the gratitude in his eyes, the quiet joy of a man who had lived to see the continuation of his faith in the next generation.

There was a quiet power in that moment. My father stood, holding Zaid in his arms, the future of our family, gazing upon the same Kaaba he had first seen decades before. This child would grow up with stories of this journey, of the grandfather who had held him so close in the most sacred of places. My father's face softened as he held Zaid, and I could see in his expression a deep, quiet contentment. It was as if, in that moment, he saw the threads of our family's faith stretching forward, linking the past with the future.

That final journey with my father was a culmination of everything he had taught me. His love for Makkah, his devotion, his sense of humility—all of it lived on in the memories we created together. The image of him, surrounded by family, with little Zaid nestled in his arms, captured the essence of our journey: the continuity of faith, the passing down of reverence, and the realization that each of us, no matter how many times we return, remains a humble servant before Allah. Standing beside him, I felt an overwhelming gratitude, not only for the gift of performing Umrah together but for the legacy of faith he had instilled in me, a legacy that would continue to guide me long after he was gone.

Performing Umrah with my father not only deepened my appreciation for our shared faith but allowed me to glimpse the beauty of worship through his eyes. It was a reminder that the journey is not only about reaching a sacred destination but about nurturing a sacred connection, one that grows stronger when shared with those we love. As we stood together in prayer, I felt an immense gratitude for these moments, for the memories we had created, and for the timeless bond of faith that would carry us forward, no matter where life might take us.

In every Tawaf, in every prayer, and in every moment of reflection, his presence, his words, and his legacy remained with me, a quiet reminder of a love for Makkah that transcended time. And with each visit to Makkah since, I am reminded that the gift of faith isn't only in our individual journeys but in the journeys we take with our loved ones—the paths we walk, the prayers we share, and the legacy of devotion that lives on through generations.

Photo by فيصل نبراوي on Unsplash (https://unsplash.com/@fmn)

CHAPTER 4

The Transformative First Hajj, 2005

My father had fulfilled his Hajj in 1983, a cherished milestone for him and our family. Since then, my mother had longed to complete her own Hajj. By 2005, the timing felt right, but she needed a companion. My eldest brother was living and working in Switzerland, so he couldn't join her. My other brother was unable to take time off from work. That's when my mother asked if I could accompany her.

It wasn't an immediate yes for me. Practical considerations like taking extra leave from my teaching role were quickly resolved, but something deeper held me back. At that point in my life, I was in a period of transition, figuring out who I was. I had just begun my TV career in 2004, presenting music shows in Hindi and Punjabi. I was a young man with blonde-streaked hair and an earring—an image more associated with modern entertainment than spiritual pilgrimage. Fame had just started to come my way within different communities. Hajj seemed to sit at odds with my public persona. However, my mother's wish mattered more than my image, and I knew I couldn't refuse her. So, I took a month off from television, promising to return to my programs after our pilgrimage.

With only my previous experience of Umrah, I set out with my mother, joining a group assembled from various parts of the UK—Newcastle, Hyde, London, Walsall, Birmingham, and others. Among them was my dear friend, Ustadh Kamal Hussain, known by many as a popular nasheed artist from Hyde. Although we were all strangers at the start, our shared journey would soon bring us closer together.

One brother in the group, whose name, sadly, I can no longer recall, became my closest companion on this trip and would ultimately have a profound impact on me.

Hajj that year was in late January, and Makkah and Madinah felt the cooler season's chill. My mother's decision to go on this particular Hajj was spurred by the fact that her eldest brother from Bangladesh was also embarking on his Hajj. For her, this was more than a pilgrimage; it was a long-awaited reunion and a journey shared with family.

Little did I know, this Hajj would change me in ways I had never anticipated. What began as a commitment to my mother would become a transformative experience, one that would shape not only my faith but the direction of my life.

To be completely honest, I was probably the least prepared person in our entire group. As I stood among seasoned pilgrims, it was hard not to feel like a novice, someone untested, stepping into an ancient tradition with only a vague sense of what lay ahead. I hadn't immersed myself in books or discussions about the journey, nor had I sought guidance from those who had walked these paths before me. I entered Hajj with nothing more than faith and a willingness to learn, trusting that Allah would see me through.

Yet, what surprised me most was the unwavering kindness of the people around me. My fellow pilgrims were patient, generous, and gentle in their guidance. They explained things I hadn't fully understood, reassured me in moments of doubt, and encouraged me when my spirits wavered. Their warmth felt like a small miracle, a mercy Allah had placed before me, because without them, I would have been entirely lost.

Arriving in Mina, I encountered challenges far beyond anything I had imagined. The vastness of the tent, filled with faces I did not know, created a sense of both closeness and anonymity that I found humbling. Each person had their own journey, their own stories and struggles. Here, we all became one, sharing not only our experiences but also the most basic of facilities, which heightened our sense of mutual dependence. The few washrooms available stretched to capacity each morning, and the long lines tested our patience. As I waited, I often thought of how this experience stripped away every layer of comfort and privacy I'd grown accustomed to. The simplicity and scarcity of resources in Mina reminded me that Hajj is not about ease but about endurance, resilience, and embracing discomfort as a form of worship. Everything here was new and unfamiliar, yet in a strange way, this shared challenge united us all, connecting us through our shared trials.

In those early days, one thought anchored me: I was here for my mother. Amidst the discomfort, uncertainty, and moments of exhaustion, my priority was her well-being. I ensured she was looked after and safe, providing what comfort I could, even in the humblest of ways. But somewhere in the back of my mind, a quiet resolve began to form—a promise that I would return for Hajj again someday, and next time, I would be fully prepared. This first pilgrimage was a powerful lesson, a necessary humbling, and though I hadn't come equipped with all the knowledge I needed, I felt that Allah had called me here for a reason.

Then came the Day of Arafat—a day I can only describe as transformative, a day unlike any other I have known. The Prophet Muhammad (PBUH) said, "Hajj is Arafat" (Sunan Ibn Majah), a reminder that standing on the plains of Arafat, completely immersed in prayer and repentance, is the heart of the pilgrimage. There, on those sacred plains, surrounded by an ocean of humanity, I found myself overcome by a profound sense of awe. The vastness of the crowd was humbling, and yet it amplified the intimacy of the moment, as if every person were alone with Allah. The heat of January was still mild, yet even the pressing warmth felt softened by the atmosphere, a sense of divine closeness enveloping us all.

Standing there, I recalled Allah's words in the Quran:

"Then when you leave Arafat, remember Allah at Al-Mash'ar al-Haram. And remember Him as He has guided you, for indeed, you were before that among those astray." (Quran 2:198)

These words resonated deeply, a reminder that we are all guided by Allah's mercy, that our paths to this moment had been uniquely prepared for us. In the hadith, the Prophet (PBUH) also says, "There is no day on which Allah frees more people from the Fire than the Day of Arafat. He comes close and expresses His pride to the angels, saying, 'What do these people want?'" (Sahih Muslim). The sheer weight of these words filled me with a sense of Allah's closeness, a realisation that this day was one of mercy beyond anything I could fathom.

Looking around, I saw faces uplifted toward the heavens, tears flowing freely as people raised their hands in supplication. There was a rawness, a vulnerability in those tears that touched me in a way I cannot fully describe. People stood there with their hearts open, their voices trembling as they poured out their deepest pleas to Allah. Each one was aware that this might be their only chance to experience Hajj, to stand as a guest of the Almighty, in absolute humility. I felt a lump rise in my throat, an overwhelming stirring within me, as I recognised the weight of this journey. It was a privilege, a gift not everyone would be granted, and here I was, standing amidst the souls of the faithful, with my mother by my side.

In that moment, I felt that Arafat was more than just a physical place; it was an experience of divine mercy, a sacred encounter where every soul was laid bare before Allah, seeking His boundless compassion. Allah had drawn close, listening to each voice, each heart. We were all united in our need for His forgiveness, and as I stood there, I could feel the weight of that mercy pressing down upon me. I left Arafat with a heart brimming with gratitude, a sense of purpose renewed, and a deep promise to return—not only to perform the rituals but to experience that divine closeness once more.

Reflecting on that day, I realised how much more meaningful it could have been if I had been truly prepared. I encourage anyone who is called to this journey to prepare in ways that extend beyond the practical. Study the rites, yes, but also prepare the heart. Engage in inner reflection, cultivate spiritual habits, and learn to be vulnerable before Allah long before you arrive. The Prophet Muhammad (PBUH) advises us, "Take provisions, for the best provision is Taqwa (consciousness of Allah)" (Quran 2:197). This is the true essence of preparing for Hajj: to bring a heart conscious of Allah, ready to be transformed by His grace.

On Arafat, I witnessed a depth of sincerity in the faces around me that revealed the heart of Hajj. Each person stood there, stripped of every pretence, emptying themselves in supplication, humbled by the opportunity to be in the presence of their Creator. I urge future pilgrims to approach Hajj as a life-altering journey, to come with full sincerity, ready to leave behind anything that weighs down the heart—pride, resentment, or attachment to the world. Hajj is a journey that demands our entirety, and only by offering ourselves fully can we hope to receive its gifts.

As the sun dipped below the horizon, marking the end of our sacred day on Arafat, the next phase of our journey began. With hearts still full of the day's blessings, we prepared to move toward Muzdalifah—a place of simplicity, humility, and spiritual intimacy with Allah. Here, the journey strips itself down to the barest essentials, calling us to embrace the purity and submission of Hajj. As prescribed, we did not pray Maghrib on Arafat, holding off in observance of the sunnah, and joined the throng of pilgrims setting out for Muzdalifah, where we would combine Maghrib and Isha upon arrival.

We boarded a coach and joined what felt like an endless line of buses, slowly inching along the road amidst a sea of pilgrims on foot. The air was filled with a mixture of anticipation and weariness as we moved forward in the dimming light, the buses progressing so slowly that it soon became clear we could have reached Muzdalifah faster if we had walked. But even this slow, uncertain journey felt deeply symbolic—another reminder of the humility required on this pilgrimage. Each pilgrim here had left behind every comfort to answer Allah's call, each small discomfort on this path a humbling reminder of our dependence on Him and how little we truly need when our hearts are full of faith.

When we finally arrived in Muzdalifah, the simplicity of the place struck me deeply. Unlike the structured tents of Mina or the grand gathering of Arafat, here there were no shelters, no barriers—only the open sky and the bare ground beneath us. The earth would be our bed, and the heavens our roof. There were no divisions, no distinctions, just pilgrims, side by side, all equal before Allah. It was a powerful, humbling sight, a reminder of our return to Allah with nothing but our deeds and our sincerity.

In Muzdalifah, we prayed Maghrib and Isha together, following the Prophet's (PBUH) guidance with one adhan and two iqamas. There was a quiet reverence as we stood together, voices rising in unison, drawing us into deeper worship and surrender. Each word of prayer felt magnified in the open air, each gesture imbued with meaning, as if the vastness of the sky above mirrored the boundless mercy of Allah stretching out over us.

After prayer, we lay down directly on the ground, without tents or coverings—just the earth beneath and the stars above. I remember lying there, wondering how I would sleep out in the open. I had never slept outside before, let alone on the bare ground with nothing to shelter me. The thought was humbling, even daunting. But as I settled in and gazed up at the stars, a deep sense of calm washed over me, as though the simplicity of that night was lifting the weight of the world from my shoulders, allowing my spirit to rest in complete surrender.

To my surprise, I fell into the deepest, most peaceful sleep I had experienced in years, as if the earth itself were cradling me. The sleep was profound, beautiful, and when I awoke for Fajr, I felt completely renewed, as if I had been restored in body and soul. I remember sharing this experience with one of the scholars in our group, expressing my amazement at the depth of my sleep. He listened, smiled knowingly, and said, "One of the signs that perhaps Allah has forgiven your sins is that on the night of Muzdalifah, you will sleep like a newborn baby—a baby that can sleep anywhere, in any condition." His words touched me deeply, filling my heart with hope and gratitude, and I felt tears gathering in my eyes.

In that moment, I realized that Muzdalifah was not merely a place of rest; it was a place of divine comfort, where Allah grants us a taste of pure peace, a glimpse of the innocence that only He can bestow. That night's sleep felt like a profound blessing, a gift that soothed not only my body but my soul. The simplicity of sleeping under the open sky, vulnerable and exposed, reminded me of our true nature before Allah—as fragile, dependent beings who, despite all else, find strength and peace only in Him.

The day after spending the night at Muzdalifah is Eid al-Adha, but during Hajj, Eid feels different from celebrations around the world. Instead of familiar family gatherings, new clothes, and festive meals, Eid at Hajj has a more introspective, solemn quality. Pilgrims are engaged in acts of deep devotion essential to completing Hajj: the stoning of Jamarat, Tawaf al-Ifadah, the cutting or shaving of hair, Qurbani (sacrificial offering), and returning to Mina for two additional nights. This day is not only spiritually profound but also physically demanding. After the night on the open ground at Muzdalifah, we journeyed to the Jamarat to perform the ritual stoning. Walking alongside my mother, I felt both the responsibility and fatigue of the days before, but the significance of the day gave us renewed strength.

The walk to the Jamarat was long and strenuous, with crowds moving like a river of pilgrims sharing in the sacred purpose. Each step grew heavier in the heat, but as we approached the Jamarat, I was reminded of Prophet Ibrahim's (AS) unwavering resolve against Shaytan's attempts to deter him. Each stone thrown at the pillar symbolized rejecting Shaytan's whispers and our dedication to Allah, casting away fears and doubts that can hinder us in life.

After stoning, we made our way to Makkah for Tawaf al-Ifadah, the ritual circling of the Kaaba that signifies closeness to Allah. The journey from Mina was tough under the sun, and I felt the strain as I supported my mother. The sight of the Kaaba upon arrival sparked a surge of energy, inspiring us through each round of Tawaf. This Tawaf was a powerful expression of submission, renewing our spiritual connection with every step.

Completing Tawaf marked another significant moment, yet there were still rites to fulfil, including the shaving of the head and the sacrificial offering. I could see the exhaustion in my mother's face, but we felt a deep sense of accomplishment and closeness to Allah. Returning to Mina for the Days of Tashreeq, we continued to stone the three Jamarat each day, a daily reminder of the struggle against temptation and our commitment to living by Allah's guidance.

The Stoning of the Jamarat: A Symbol of Faith and Resistance

Among the rites, stoning the Jamarat, particularly the largest, Jamrat al-Aqabah, is deeply symbolic. This act re-enacts the story of Prophet Ibrahim (AS) and his son Ismail (AS), embodying submission, sacrifice, and resilience against temptation. When Allah commanded Ibrahim (AS) to sacrifice his beloved son, Ismail (AS) accepted with steadfast faith, saying: "O my father, do as you are commanded. You will find me, if Allah wills, steadfast" (Quran 37:102). Shaytan appeared three times to dissuade them, but each time Ibrahim rejected his whispers by casting stones, symbolizing unwavering faith over doubt.

Upon returning to Mina, we spent the next two days focused on the stoning ritual, an essential and symbolic act of Hajj. Each morning, we walked to the Jamarat, performing the stoning at all three pillars, symbolizing our rejection of Shaytan and his temptations. The final stoning marked the completion of these rites and with it, the conclusion of Hajj. The feeling was bittersweet, a profound sense of accomplishment mingled with the awareness that this transformative journey was coming to an end. After completing the rites, we prepared to make our way back to Makkah, where the Haram waited for our concluding prayers.

On that last day, we left our camp shortly after Zuhr prayers, with the aim of reaching the Haram in Makkah by Asr. There was a peculiar stillness in the air, and the sky was a rare sight for this desert land—heavy with rain clouds. Although rainfall has become more common in recent years, it was still a surprise to see such overcast skies in Saudi Arabia. The clouds hung low, casting a hushed, sombre tone over the pilgrims as they moved through the streets of Makkah.

As we approached our lodging in Makkah, a light drizzle began to fall. The rain was gentle at first, a refreshing coolness after days under the relentless sun. I quickly deposited our bags and took my mother to the Haram so we could join the Asr prayers in congregation. By the time we reached the masjid, the rain had intensified, a rare and almost surreal experience for such a sacred and dry land.

I settled my mother in the women's section, which was slightly elevated above the mataf, the open area around the

Kaaba reserved for tawaf. I joined the congregation for Asr, the air thick with the scent of rain mingling with the solemn reverence of thousands of worshippers. By the third rakah of Asr, I could feel water pooling around my ankles. With each rakah, the rain continued, and by the time we entered the fourth rakah, the mataf was awash, and we found ourselves making sujood in water. The experience was humbling—a reminder of Allah's power over all things. It felt as though the rain itself was part of our prayer, a physical manifestation of purity and mercy.

After the prayer, I hurried back to find my mother. We left the Haram and began making our way back to our lodging in Shamea. As we reached the main road, I realized it had transformed into a small river; the rainwater was flowing steadily, making it difficult to cross. We waited, watching the water slowly recede, and when it was finally manageable, we crossed carefully, supporting each other as we walked. Alhamdulillah, we made it back safe and sound, grateful for the shelter and warmth that awaited us.

As we settled back into our lodging, my mind turned to the other pilgrims who were still in Mina. I imagined the camps, typically bustling with activity, now soaked by the unexpected rains. Later, I learned that the heavy rain had caused significant disruptions in Mina, with reports that two pilgrims had tragically lost their lives, and nearly 200 others suffered injuries, mainly fractures, due to falls in the slippery conditions. Roads had become congested as traffic slowed, with camps flooding and many pilgrims stranded, waiting for the waters to subside.

This rare rainfall during Hajj was both a reminder of nature's unpredictability and a test of endurance and patience for those still in Mina. The rains highlighted how even in the face of challenging conditions, the devotion of the pilgrims remained steadfast, each one determined to fulfill the rites of Hajj, despite the hardships. It was a humbling conclusion to our journey, reminding us of the resilience required to undertake such a sacred path and of Allah's mercy in all conditions.

Our Final Days of Hajj in Madinah

We spent our last days of Hajj in Madinah, and the city's calmness was a striking contrast to the bustling atmosphere of Makkah. The weather was colder than I had expected, and I even bought a jumper to stay warm during Fajr prayers. My mother, especially eager to perform Hajj this year, was motivated in part by the fact that her elder brother had also come from Bangladesh for the pilgrimage. Although we had a brief meeting with him in Makkah before departing for Mina, we were unable to find him during the key rites in Mina, Arafat, or Muzdalifah.

On our second day in Madinah, as I was walking my mother to the Haram, she began talking about her brother. She wondered aloud where he might be staying and if we would see him again. Since he didn't have a mobile phone and we didn't know his accommodations in Madinah, finding him felt unlikely. But, almost miraculously, just as those words left my mother's lips, I looked up and saw my uncle walking toward the masjid, a little ahead of us. My mother was overjoyed—her heartfelt desire to see him again had been answered almost instantly. This unexpected encounter felt like a blessed moment, a reminder of the power of sincere supplication, and it left a lasting impression on us both.

The friend who's name i have forgotten – but his advice still remains an important landmark in my life.

During Hajj, I met a young brother from Hyde, whose name I can no longer recall, as we lost touch over 15 years ago. But despite the years that have passed, the impact of our brief friendship remains vivid in my heart. We connected during the days spent in Makkah, Mina, and Madinah. He was around my age yet carried a quiet wisdom that I often turned to, and his words seemed to reach something deep within me.

On our final day in Madinah, as we sat outside Masjid Nabawi with the light fading before Maghrib, there was a stillness between us. Just moments before the adhan, he turned to me with a gentle seriousness.

"Brother Rizwan," he said softly, "tomorrow we'll go back to the UK, back to our lives and routines. I hope we can keep in touch, but before we leave, I have something I want to say."

He paused, as if choosing each word carefully. "In our time together, I noticed how people from different communities in the UK recognized you. I overheard someone say, 'Look, there's the guy from TV... has he become Muslim?'" His words struck a chord. I hadn't given much thought to how people saw me or what that might mean, but he looked at me with a sincerity that made me listen closely. "Being recognized can be a blessing, a chance to do something good. Alhamdulillah, you have a following. Imagine if people knew you, not for music, but for something better, something that would bring them closer to Allah?"

I felt my heart stirring as he continued, "Why don't you make an intention here and now, in Madinah, just before Maghrib, that when you return, you'll leave behind the world of music and TV presenting and use the gifts Allah has given you for da'wah. I know it won't be easy, but we're in a place where duas are answered. I'm saying this as a genuine brother who believes there's something greater you can achieve."

His words went straight to my soul, as though he had seen something in me that I had been blind to. He was asking me to let go of the path I knew, to embrace a calling greater than recognition or success. I didn't have to think twice. In that moment, I felt the presence of the sacred city around us, the air heavy with the blessings of Maghrib in Madinah. I looked up to the sky, and from the depths of my heart, I made an intention: 'Oh Allah, allow me to return and change things for the better. If there is a higher purpose for me, guide me to it. I promise to leave all that I know as soon as I return home'.

That moment transformed me, as if a door I hadn't known existed had suddenly opened. With Madinah's blessings surrounding us, I felt a resolve I hadn't felt before—a clarity that, whatever awaited me back home, I was ready to walk the path that would bring me closer to Allah.

Perhaps that moment was the turning point, the beginning of a journey that would shape my life and lead me to where I am now, writing these reflections. Looking back, I realise how much his words stayed with me, stirring something in my heart that, at the time, I couldn't fully understand. Yet those words lingered, a seed that would grow over the years, guiding me to seek a purpose beyond myself. I often wonder if he knew the impact he had on me, or if he sensed the depth of his advice as we sat there, with the blessed air of Madinah surrounding us.

I will forever be grateful to that brother, who, with a few sincere words, helped me see a different path. There's a part of me that holds onto the hope that one day, he might come across this book, recognize these memories, and reach out. I would want him to know how deeply his words took root, how much they helped me realign my life with the principles of faith. His friendship reminds me of the wisdom of the Prophet Muhammad (PBUH), who said, "A person is upon the religion of his close friend, so let one of you look at whom he befriends." (Sunan Abu Dawood).

Wherever that brother may be, I pray that Allah blesses him with all the goodness in this world and the next. May he be rewarded for the sincerity in his heart and the kindness in his words. And may he know, somehow, the immense impact he left behind. Aameen.

Was my du'a' in Madinah answered?

Returning to London after Hajj, I felt an undeniable shift within me. Contractually, I still had to finish a few more weeks on my TV program, but my heart wasn't in it anymore. My sense of purpose had changed, and I found myself eager to part ways with that world. I knew I had some talent for TV presenting, but now I wanted to use it differently. Yet, the options seemed slim. Islam Channel, the leading Islamic network in the UK, had just launched about six months earlier, but I was certain they wouldn't consider me. My previous work was known for a very different style—one that clashed with their values.

But Allah is the best of planners. A few weeks later, while visiting my parents in Loughborough, my sister came to me with a request. She, her husband, and some friends had tickets for an Islamic conference in Manchester—the Unity Conference—and they needed someone to drive a minibus. I wasn't busy, so I agreed, planning to drop them off, wander around, and pick them up later.

When the day came, I drove them to the venue, let them out, and was about to leave when I heard a knock on my window. Rolling it down, I found a brother smiling warmly. "Are you the guy from TV? My mum's a big fan! What brings you here?" he asked. I explained that I was just the driver today, here to drop off my family. "You're leaving?" he asked, surprised. I told him I didn't have a ticket, and I hadn't planned to attend. His face lit up. "Brother Rizwan, park up and come with me," he insisted. "I'm one of the organizers, Sabooh. I work for Islam Channel. I'll arrange a backstage pass for you, so you won't feel out of place in the main auditorium."

His offer felt like a nudge from Allah. He even promised lunch, so I agreed and followed him inside. He led me to a spacious room set up for guest speakers, with lunch laid out. He guided me to a seat beside a man I didn't recognize—a man in a suit and cap who greeted me warmly. Out of courtesy, I asked him what he did, and we exchanged polite conversation. But mostly, I watched the room, observing the lively exchanges between the speakers and guests.

As lunch wrapped up, the conference was set to begin, and the first speaker took the stage. Sabooh found me a chair just behind the curtains where I could listen without being visible in the main area. I settled in and listened, captivated by the speaker's voice as it filled the auditorium. His words were electric, each one reaching into the deepest parts of my heart. His message stirred something in me that had lain dormant, an urgency to change, to redirect my path towards something that felt truer and more aligned with my intentions from Hajj. I had to know who he was.

When he finished, he returned backstage, and I realized it was the same man I'd sat next to at lunch. He extended his hand with a smile. "I'm Zakir... Zakir Naik. Dr. Zakir Naik."

The name hit me like a lightning bolt. Here was one of the most respected voices in the world of Islamic knowledge, a man whose lectures reached millions, seated right beside me, speaking words that struck straight to my soul. Meeting him wasn't a coincidence. This was a clear answer to the du'a I had made in Madinah—a sign from Allah, showing me a way forward that I hadn't yet considered. I felt a newfound certainty: the path I was meant to take wasn't the one I had been on.

That chance encounter—the drive to Manchester, the invitation backstage, the stirring words of Dr. Zakir Naik—set everything into motion. I knew, without a doubt, that Allah had placed me there. He had brought me to that conference, to that very moment, to reignite the intention I'd made in Madinah and to open a door I hadn't even dared to knock on. This was my calling. And every step since then has been a testament to that answered du'a, a journey towards something far more profound.

After Dr. Zakir Naik's inspiring lecture, Sabooh found me, smiling as he asked, "Did you enjoy that?" I was still lost in thought, moved by what I'd just heard, and barely managed to thank him. Sabooh then handed me his business card and said, "Next Wednesday, come visit us at the channel. Just stop by and see the setup—I'm sure many of my colleagues would love to meet you." His invitation caught me off guard, but I accepted with a grateful heart.

The following week, with a mixture of anticipation and curiosity, I found myself at Islam Channel's offices on Bonhill Street, not far from Liverpool Street. As I waited in the reception area, I saw a group of young people around my age chatting and laughing together. This lively team was behind the channel that had quickly become a staple in Muslim households across the UK, delivering content that resonated with so many.

Before long, a young man named Arfan approached me with a warm handshake and a welcoming smile. His genuine kindness surprised me. As he guided me through the office, he chatted easily, mentioning that he'd heard a lot about me from Sabooh and that some of his own family members recognized me from TV. We eventually settled into two chairs, exchanged a few polite questions about family, and then he asked the question that stopped me in my tracks.

"Have you ever considered joining Islam Channel?"

I was taken aback. I hesitated, explaining that I had been known for presenting music programs and wasn't sure how I would fit in with their vision. Arfan's response was even more surprising. He said, "What if you take some time to think of a concept for a program, and give me a call next week? See how you feel about it."

I agreed, still in shock at the speed of it all. Allah's plan was unfolding faster than I could have anticipated.

Over the next week, I wrestled with ideas, trying to imagine what type of program I could create that would bring people together in an uplifting, meaningful way. One morning, it struck me—a lightbulb moment. In my previous TV role, I'd often encouraged people to sing in a game of musical knowledge, a fun and interactive style. What if I adapted that style to a program based on Quran recitation? A friendly competition centred around something truly meaningful.

And so, the concept for 'NQC – National Qiraat Competition' was born. The program quickly took shape, and with Islam Channel's support, it went on to become a flagship show, one I was privileged to present for 10 seasons. The series became a treasured platform, with spectacular finales held at the Global Peace & Unity (GPU) events at London's Excel, bringing people together in an environment of faith and unity.

In those early days, I was blessed with a co-presenter and judge who became an invaluable support—a man who embodied the values of dedication and sincerity. The first judge on NQC was none other than the legendary Imam Qasim. His presence brought wisdom and guidance to the show, and I'll always remember his contribution. May Allah bless him for the tireless work he does around the world.

Reflecting on that journey, I'm overwhelmed by how Allah's plan unfolded, far beyond anything I could have envisioned. From a chance encounter in Manchester to a life-changing invitation from Islam Channel, I found myself on a path I hadn't even known existed, all sparked by a simple du'a in Madinah. Allah truly is the best of planners, guiding us when we're ready—even if we don't yet know it.

The shortest Umrah trip

In 2005, I had transitioned from my career in teaching to a new chapter at Islam Channel, working as a programme's producer and presenter. One day, as I was immersed in the usual tasks, I was unexpectedly called into the CEO's office. Mohammed Ali Harrath, the CEO, looked at me and asked, "Would you like to go to Umrah?" The question caught me by surprise, but my answer was obvious—how could I possibly say no?

At that time, British Midland Airways, known as BMI (and which sadly ceased operations in 2019), had just launched a new direct route from London to Jeddah. To promote the route, they wanted to invite members from the community to experience it firsthand. Around 20 of us were chosen to fly to Jeddah, with a two-day stopover in Makkah, capped off with a launch reception at the British Embassy in Jeddah. For me, it wasn't just a chance to experience a new route; it was another blessed opportunity to lay my eyes upon the Ka'bah.

Representing Islam Channel, Khurram Zuberi—my dear friend and colleague at the time—and I set off on this unique journey. Makkah in 2005 was a city in transition, where the old world and the new seemed to converge. Much of Makkah's original landscape was still intact. Two large mountains, which stood where the imposing clock tower now resides, were in the process of being levelled, marking the beginning of a transformation that would alter the skyline of Makkah forever.

On this occasion, we were accommodated at the Makkah Makarim Ajyad Hotel, a charming, classic five-star hotel located on Ajyad Street. The hotel held a certain nostalgic allure, a reminder of Makkah's character before the wave of modern skyscrapers. Unlike today, the Haram was relatively quiet, and the crowds were sparse, allowing us to perform Umrah with ease. The peaceful atmosphere gave us a rare, undisturbed connection to the sacred rituals.

After completing Umrah, I returned to the hotel, feeling the tranquillity that only such a spiritual experience can bring. Just then, I received a message that my sister had given birth to her first child, my nephew. The joy of this news added a special layer to the memory, making it one of those moments forever etched in my mind.

CHAPTER 5

The Working Hajj

After my first Hajj, a sense of incompleteness lingered. I had entered that journey unprepared, and while I had fulfilled my obligations, something in me craved a deeper connection, a chance to experience it again with true understanding. But returning for Hajj wasn't easy. Hajj is a significant financial commitment, and at the time, I was working part-time at Islam Channel while dedicating nearly 80% of my time to various charitable projects. That work, as meaningful as it was, filled my weeks then as it still does today.

In 2005, Islam Channel made history by broadcasting Hajj live to audiences across the UK. I remember watching that first broadcast, utterly mesmerised. The scenes of pilgrims circling the Ka'bah, standing in Arafat, moving between Mina and Muzdalifah—all unfolding live—felt almost surreal. Hajj, once an experience distant to those who couldn't go, was now right there on our screens. It felt as though we were witnessing a piece of heaven on earth. As I sat there watching, I made a heartfelt prayer, "Ya Allah, give me the opportunity to be a part of something so profound, to inspire others to make this journey."

Little did I know then that Allah had already begun to answer my prayer. Soon, I was invited to join Islam Channel's live Hajj broadcast team, combining my role as a producer and presenter with the chance to perform Hajj again. In fact, over the years, I would be blessed to perform Hajj seven times through this role. I came to call these journeys my "working Hajj."

Each year, the Saudi Ministry of Culture and Information invited media representatives from around the world to cover Hajj. This invitation extended to television networks, radio broadcasters, print journalists, and other dignitaries. As guests of the Ministry, our team experienced Hajj with unique privileges, structured differently from the typical pilgrim's journey. Our visas were issued as journalists and broadcasters, allowing us smoother access through immigration and offering specific permissions during the pilgrimage itself. But these privileges came with great responsibilities, and we faced our own set of challenges.

Our team typically consisted of about ten people: cameramen, a satellite engineer, an editor, a producer, and me as the presenter. We'd arrive in Jeddah carrying an immense load of broadcasting equipment essential for live coverage. Boxes of cameras, satellite dishes, editing equipment, lighting—our baggage was more than just personal belongings; it was the tools required to capture and relay Hajj's story to viewers back home. The Ministry hosted us for the five critical days of Hajj, but for the remainder of our stay, we were responsible for our accommodations.

We usually found ourselves in a modest hotel or house high on a hill, strategically chosen to ensure a direct line for our satellite connection with the Haram in the backdrop. These places were not always accessible by car, so our team would physically haul all the gear up steep, winding paths. Carrying heavy equipment uphill in the scorching Makkah heat, often while in Ihram, was no small feat. But we were united by a sense of purpose: we were here not only to perform our own Hajj but also to bring Hajj to those who couldn't be there in person.

After finally settling in, the real work would begin. Within hours of our arrival, we'd set up the satellite, assemble cameras, test connections, and prepare for our first live broadcast. Amid the hustle of setting up, I'd sneak away with some team members to perform Umrah. We'd walk to the Haram in awe, fully aware of the blessing to be there, even if only briefly, and complete our tawaf and sa'i as quickly as we could before rushing back to make sure everything was ready for the broadcast.

When we went live, I felt the weight of my role in a way I had never experienced before. As the presenter, I was on air for hours, standing in the blistering Makkah sun, narrating the scenes of Hajj for viewers. The intensity of the midday heat was unforgiving, and it would leave us drained. We'd break for a short rest, then return for the evening broadcast, often finishing around 1 a.m., exhausted but filled with a unique sense of satisfaction. My words, I hoped, would convey the experience of Hajj to those watching, letting them feel a part of the journey even from miles away.

But our responsibilities didn't end with the live broadcasts. By day, we would begin filming for the "Footsteps" documentary, a feature capturing the stages of Hajj, from Mina to Arafat, Muzdalifah, and beyond. The team and I would travel to each of these sacred sites, filming the rituals, the faces of the pilgrims, the emotional scenes as millions of believers stood together in prayer. We knew the weight of what we were creating. Each day, our editor worked tirelessly to craft the footage into a compelling segment, ready to be broadcast by that evening. The long hours and tight schedules took their toll, but it was worth every moment.

After five days of intense, non-stop coverage, we'd pack up the equipment, barely giving ourselves time to rest, and prepare for the most anticipated part of the journey: the days of Hajj itself. Our first stop was always Mina, and as we joined the flow of millions of pilgrims, the intensity of our work merged with the essence of worship. In the heart of this massive congregation, surrounded by voices raised in prayer, I felt the exhaustion fade away, replaced by a profound sense of gratitude.

This "working Hajj" was unlike any other pilgrimage. It demanded physical endurance, patience, and an unwavering commitment to the mission. But it also gave me something rare: a blend of duty and devotion, an experience where my work became an extension of my worship, and my worship a testament to the work we were doing. These journeys taught me the extraordinary privilege of merging one's faith with one's mission, creating a lasting legacy that would inspire others to take this journey for themselves.

The five days we spent as guests of the Saudi Ministry of Culture and Information during Hajj were an experience unlike any other. In a way, this arrangement allowed us to perform Hajj while fulfilling our duty to broadcast the experience to millions. Each year, the Ministry provided a designated transport service to take us from Makkah to the media compound in Mina, where journalists and media teams from around the world gathered to cover this sacred event.

The media compound was strategically located close to the Jamarat, the site of the symbolic stoning of the devil, which meant we had a front-row vantage point of one of the most critical rites of Hajj. The compound itself was set up almost like a small village, with rows of what felt like container homes, each allocated to a different media team. These units were simple and functional, equipped only with the most basic amenities, perhaps to preserve the essence of Mina's tented city and to remind us of the equality and simplicity that are central to the Hajj experience.

Each unit offered just enough space for our team to rest briefly, stow our belongings, and prepare for the next broadcast. There was no luxury here, only the essentials—a reminder that the heart of Hajj is not in the material, but in the sincerity of worship. Despite the simplicity, there was a certain comfort in being close to the other media teams, with everyone sharing the same facilities, united in a common mission to relay the spirit of Hajj to audiences around the world.

Above the compound was a flat rooftop that quickly became one of our main broadcasting hubs. From there, we had an aerial view of Mina, the vast sea of white tents stretching as far as the eye could see, and, in the distance, the massive Jamarat structure. This elevated perspective was ideal for capturing the enormity of Mina and the energy of the pilgrims as they moved in waves toward the Jamarat, each one intent on fulfilling this essential ritual.

Upon arrival, the first task was always to unload and unpack our equipment. Cameras, lights, microphones, editing tools, and, of course, the satellite gear—each piece needed careful handling and precise setup. We carried everything up to the rooftop, where our team assembled a makeshift mini studio that became our command centre for the broadcasts. Aligning the satellite dish was a meticulous job, especially with the intense heat and crowds all around. It required patience and teamwork to ensure we had a strong, stable connection to bring this experience live to viewers. Unloading and setting up our equipment in the media compound was already a strenuous task but doing it all in ihram added an entirely new layer of challenge. The ihram, with its two simple white cloths, was designed for simplicity and humility, stripping away all distinctions of wealth and status, but it was not the most practical attire for carrying heavy equipment and navigating the rooftop setup. Each member of our team—from the satellite engineer to the cameramen, producer, and myself as the presenter—was clothed in ihram, embodying the spirit of Hajj, yet also mindful of the physical limitations it imposed.

In ihram, every movement demanded extra care. With no pockets and no belt, we had to be resourceful in managing our tools, cables, and personal items, balancing them as we manoeuvred equipment up the steep stairs to the rooftop. Each step felt heavier, and each piece of equipment we lifted felt more cumbersome under the hot sun and amidst the thick crowds. The simple sandals we wore often felt unsteady on the stairs and rooftops, and it was a task just to keep the ihram cloths properly wrapped while we were climbing ladders, adjusting cables, or securing the satellite dish.

This extra effort, though physically taxing, also deepened our connection to the purpose of the journey. There was something humbling and profoundly spiritual about setting up the broadcast equipment in ihram, especially as we paused to look out over the sprawling tents of Mina and the continuous movement of pilgrims below. Our attire was a constant reminder that, despite our roles as media professionals, we were also among those millions, standing equal before Allah, part of the sacred brotherhood of pilgrims.

In these moments, I felt an intensified sense of purpose. Our work was difficult, yes, but our ihram served as a reminder of the responsibility we held—not only to our audience back home but to the values of Hajj itself. Every connection we tightened, every piece of equipment we assembled, every moment we went live was an act of service, an offering to bring the beauty, unity, and reverence of Hajj into homes around the world.

The strain of working in ihram only heightened the sacredness of the experience. It wasn't merely a job or an assignment; it was a way of living out the very humility and devotion that Hajj required. And as I spoke into the camera, sharing the scenes unfolding around us, I hoped that our viewers could feel a part of that sacredness, a part of the brotherhood and sisterhood that Hajj inspires, across every boundary and from every corner of the world.

Once everything was in place, we would begin broadcasting, standing on that rooftop overlooking Mina. The setup may have been temporary, but the mission felt timeless. As I spoke into the camera, I was acutely aware of the privilege of being there—not only to perform Hajj but to share its message with countless others who could only dream of making this journey. With every word, I hoped to convey a sense of the awe, humility, and unity I felt standing among the millions who had gathered to fulfil their sacred duty.

Each day, as the pilgrims moved to different locations, we packed up and relocated our equipment, following them to capture each moment. It was exhausting work, but standing on that rooftop, overlooking the sprawling tents of Mina and the throngs of pilgrims, was a reminder of the incredible scope of Hajj and the honour of sharing it with the world.

No sooner had we completed the entire broadcast setup for our first night in Mina than we found ourselves packing it all up again, preparing to move to another media compound in Arafat. It was an intense, back-to-back process, demanding that we dismantle and repack each piece of equipment swiftly, knowing we'd soon have to rebuild it all from scratch in a new location.

The Arafat compound, situated in the heart of the sacred plain, offered us a stunning, elevated view of the vast landscape. From this vantage point, we could see Masjid Namira standing with its grand presence, Jabal Al Rahma reaching up as a focal point of the pilgrimage, and the seemingly endless expanse of pilgrims gathered on the plains. It was an awe-inspiring sight, one that reminded us of the magnitude of the Day of Arafat—a day when millions stand united, pleading to Allah in the most heartfelt moments of the Hajj journey.

As we set up our equipment here, the view lent a sense of urgency and reverence to our work. We were no longer simply documenting an event; we were bearing witness to the core of Hajj, the very essence of what brought millions of hearts to these plains. The elevated view allowed us to capture not just the individuals, but the collective devotion, the sweeping scenes of pilgrims standing, praying, and reflecting on their connection with Allah, all set against the timeless beauty of Arafat.

The broadcast on the Day of Arafat was often the most challenging and demanding of the entire Hajj experience. This day required an unbroken, continuous live feed, stretching from the early hours of dawn until sunset, capturing the profound atmosphere of Arafat. As presenters, we took turns at the forefront, each of us standing before the camera, narrating the scenes, relaying reflections, and sharing the significance of this monumental day with viewers back home. Between our stints on camera, we found precious moments to retreat for our own private ibadah, slipping away from the rooftop to engage in personal prayers, reciting Qur'an, and making du'a, aware of the enormous spiritual weight of this day.

The physical conditions, however, were far from easy. Broadcasting from an exposed rooftop, there was no shelter from the intense sun that beat down relentlessly, amplifying the scorching midday heat. Dressed in ihram, we felt the sun bearing down on our uncovered heads, and the sweat ran freely as we focused on our work, each of us acutely aware of the toll it took. Yet, in that physical strain lay a profound reminder of the deeper purpose of Arafat. Standing under the blazing sun, drenched in sweat and striving to communicate the spirit of the day, brought us face-to-face with the humbling reality that this was only a small taste of the ultimate gathering on Yaum al-Qiyamah, the Day of Judgment.

On that day, we will all stand in a heat far greater than Arafat's, awaiting our fate, hoping for Allah's mercy and forgiveness. The discomfort and fatigue we felt on Arafat day weren't merely challenges to overcome—they were, in a way, an embodiment of what Arafat itself symbolizes: humility, endurance, and the stripping away of worldly comforts as we present ourselves before Allah. The sweat, the sunburn, and the weariness became reminders of our shared human vulnerability and the fleeting nature of life's comforts. We felt ourselves not just reporting on Arafat, but in a small way, experiencing the essence of it.

Each time we returned to the broadcast, we felt more connected, our voices carrying both the weight of the day's message and the reality of the experience. We were not just narrators; we were participants in Arafat's journey, sharing not only what we saw but what we felt. And with each prayer we offered between broadcasts, we joined the millions on those sacred plains, standing shoulder to shoulder in our yearning for forgiveness, praying that the day's struggle would not be in vain. The hope was that, through our efforts both on and off camera, we would convey the soul of Arafat to those watching and that Allah, in His infinite mercy, would look upon us all with compassion and grant us His forgiveness.

The Day of Arafat holds an unparalleled significance in the pilgrimage of Hajj, marking the spiritual peak of the journey and a day that epitomizes Allah's mercy and forgiveness. As we stood on that rooftop, broadcasting live under the intense sun, we were constantly reminded that this was no ordinary day. The Prophet Muhammad (PBUH) said, "Hajj is Arafat" (Tirmidhi), underscoring that without standing on Arafat, Hajj is incomplete. This day is the very heart of the pilgrimage, where millions gather in unity, humility, and supplication, embodying the essence of submission to Allah.

Our broadcasts sought to convey this to the viewers at home—that the Day of Arafat is a day of unparalleled spiritual opportunity, a day unlike any other in the entire year. The Prophet (PBUH) also said, "There is no day on which Allah frees more people from the Fire than the Day of Arafat" (Sahih Muslim). This reminder weighed heavily on our hearts, for we were not just presenting the scenes of Arafat, but participating in them, knowing that this was a time when Allah's mercy flows boundlessly. Every moment on Arafat was a precious chance for repentance, a time when, as the hadith assures us, Allah draws near to His servants, looks upon those who stand on Arafat with compassion, and forgives them.

In the Qur'an, Allah speaks directly about the Day of Arafat, highlighting the importance of this blessed gathering. In Surah Al-Baqarah (2:198), He says: "But when you depart from Arafat, remember Allah at Al-Mash'ar Al-Haram. And remember Him, as He has guided you, for indeed, you were before that among those astray." This verse directs pilgrims to remember Allah as they depart from Arafat, emphasising that this day is one of remembrance, repentance, and conscious awareness of His guidance. Arafat is a physical reminder that, as we leave, we should carry with us a deep sense of His guidance, which brought us to this place of forgiveness and reflection.

As we broadcasted the scenes of pilgrims on the vast plains, raising their hands in heartfelt supplication, the significance of this day became almost palpable. On Arafat, the unity of the Muslim Ummah is powerfully displayed. The Prophet (PBUH) delivered his Farewell Sermon on this very day, standing before the masses to declare the finality of his message, urging equality, justice, and unity. His words, as narrated, "O people, your blood and your wealth are sacred...," resonate with the principles of compassion and justice, values we broadcasted to remind viewers that Arafat is not just an act of worship but a symbol of the universal values of Islam.

In our moments away from the camera, we stood with the other pilgrims on those blessed plains, experiencing Arafat's profound call for forgiveness, unity, and submission. We recited du'as and sought Allah's mercy, knowing that every moment on Arafat was a chance for renewal. The words of the Prophet (PBUH) echoed in our hearts: "The best supplication is the supplication on the day of Arafat" (Muwatta, Malik). We prayed fervently, aware that Allah was nearer to us on this day, listening and responding to the pleas of every servant who called upon Him.

And with each broadcast, we hoped to share not only the sights of Arafat but its soul—the profound sense of hope, the vastness of Allah's mercy, and the reminder that, on this day, every person's sincere repentance is a step closer to Allah's forgiveness. Standing under the heat of Arafat, broadcasting these scenes, we became more than witnesses; we were humbled participants in a day that reaches beyond time, space, and circumstance, binding us in our humanity and faith, reminding us that Allah's mercy is always within reach, as long as we stand before Him in sincerity and humility.

As we concluded the intense and spiritually charged broadcast from Arafat, the media representatives and journalists, like all other pilgrims, began the journey to Muzdalifah. The transition marked a shift from the intense focus of Arafat's prayers to the simplicity and humility of

Muzdalifah. Unlike the compound in Arafat, the Muzdalifah site was not set up for broadcasting; it was purely a place to rest, to reflect, and to fulfil the rites of Hajj. We were no longer in front of cameras or on-air. Instead, like the millions of pilgrims around us, we were simply here to carry out the next steps of the pilgrimage.

The compound in Muzdalifah was basic, an open enclosure that offered us shelter under the vast, star-studded sky. No tents, no roofs—just a stretch of ground where everyone lay side by side, a sea of white-clad pilgrims resting directly on the earth. This openness reminded us of the profound equality in Hajj: all of us, regardless of background or status, were united under the same night sky, sharing the same ground, and in this simplicity, seeking Allah's acceptance. Laying there on the earth in our ihram, we could see the stars as they glittered above, offering a moment of peace after the intensity of the Day of Arafat.

Muzdalifah is also where pilgrims gather pebbles for the ritual stoning of the Jamarat, symbolising our commitment to resist temptation and reject evil. Walking around the open grounds, we carefully selected our stones, mindful of their significance. Each pebble felt small and ordinary, yet it carried a weighty purpose for the days ahead. The act of collecting these stones was both humbling and empowering—a reminder of our intention to strive for goodness and reject the whispers of wrongdoing. The simplicity of the act, the quiet under the night sky, the occasional murmur of fellow pilgrims—all contributed to an atmosphere of shared purpose and introspection.

After spending a significant portion of the night in Muzdalifah, we found brief moments of rest, appreciating the stillness around us. The exhaustion of the day melted into a sense of serene anticipation. As dawn approached, we prepared to journey back to Mina, where the next day's rituals awaited us. The transition from Arafat to Muzdalifah, and now back to Mina, felt like a series of profound steps, each bringing us closer to the essence of Hajj.

Returning to Mina, we carried with us the pebbles, the memories of Arafat, and the humility of Muzdalifah, ready to continue the rites of Hajj, which were not just physical actions but deeply spiritual commitments that marked our journey of self-reflection, devotion, and transformation.

Back in Mina, we once again set up the broadcast equipment, ready to cover the coming three days of Hajj. The task was physically demanding, as this broadcast would span all day and all night, capturing every aspect of the pilgrimage. Our elevated position in the media compound, perched high on the side of a mountain, offered us a unique vantage point. From this height, we had a sweeping view of the Jamarat below—a sight that symbolized the critical next steps of Hajj—as well as the sprawling tent city of Mina, where millions of pilgrims gathered. Directly beneath us lay Masjid Al-Khaif, a sacred mosque that held deep significance, as it is said that 'over seventy prophets prayed' within its walls.

Masjid Al-Khaif is not just a mosque but a landmark with rich historical and spiritual significance. The Prophet Muhammad (PBUH) is reported to have prayed there, and according to hadith, seventy prophets before him also prayed in this mosque, imbuing it with a timeless sanctity. Pilgrims flock here, drawn by its history and its connection to the prophets, adding to the collective atmosphere of devotion that permeates Mina. Observing the throngs of people around Masjid Al-Khaif from our elevated position served as a constant reminder of the continuity of faith across generations, connecting us all through the same acts of worship.

The next day would be Eid al-Adha, marking one of the most significant days of the Hajj journey. Like all pilgrims, we would be observing several essential rites, each symbolizing different aspects of submission and faith. Between our broadcasting duties, our team made preparations to head back to Makkah to perform Tawaf al-Ifadah, an obligatory circumambulation of the Ka'bah that signifies the deepened connection to Allah and completes the essential rites of Hajj. Tawaf al-Ifadah is a critical act of devotion, performed in the heart of Makkah, and for many, it's a moment of spiritual realization as they circle the Ka'bah, embodying the unity and submission central to Hajj.

In addition to Tawaf, we also observed Qurbani (the sacrificial offering), honouring the legacy of Prophet Ibrahim (AS) and his willingness to sacrifice for Allah's sake. This act of sacrifice is more than ritual; it symbolizes the pilgrims' readiness to surrender their attachments and worldly desires in devotion to Allah. After completing the sacrifice, pilgrims proceed to shorten or shave their heads, known as Halq (shaving) or Taqsir (shortening). For men, shaving the head represents a form of humility and a fresh start, shedding the past to emerge renewed in faith.

After fulfilling these rituals in Makkah, we returned to Mina to continue the day's rites. One of the key rituals on this day was the stoning of the Jamarat, specifically the largest of the three pillars. Each stone represents an act of defiance against temptation and evil, reenacting Prophet Ibrahim's resistance to the devil's whispers. Pilgrims throw seven pebbles at the pillar, symbolizing the rejection of sin and reaffirming their commitment to Allah's path. As we stood on the rooftop of the media compound, watching the steady stream of pilgrims moving toward the Jamarat below, we were reminded of the strength of faith required to resist temptation and maintain one's resolve.

For our team, Eid al-Adha was a test of endurance and commitment. Between the broadcasts, we made every effort to fulfil our own Hajj obligations, running back and forth from Mina to Makkah and returning in time to resume the broadcast. It was a physically and spiritually demanding day, balancing the intense workload with the profound personal responsibilities of Hajj. Despite the challenges, each completed ritual infused us with renewed energy and a deepened sense of purpose.

The broadcasts continued throughout the day and night, capturing the pilgrims' journeys, their moments of prayer and reflection, and the essence of Eid al-Adha. Watching and sharing these scenes was humbling; we were not just documenting an event but bearing witness to acts of faith that transcended time, culture, and language. With each broadcast, we hoped to share a glimpse of the devotion we witnessed with those watching from afar, connecting them, in spirit, to the pilgrimage's powerful message of faith, sacrifice, and unity.

For the next two days, our work continued nonstop, with day and night broadcasts capturing the ebb and flow of Hajj's final stages. Between live segments, we were constantly filming, editing, and broadcasting short documentaries, each one created in real-time. These documentaries took us deep into the heart of the pilgrimage—into the crowded tents of Mina, to the symbolic stoning at the Jamarat, and to the faces of pilgrims as they shared their thoughts, emotions, and reflections on this life-changing journey.

In the camps, we captured the camaraderie and resilience of pilgrims who, though exhausted, found strength and community in each other's presence. The air was thick with gratitude, as pilgrims recounted their experiences, many moved to tears by the journey's spiritual magnitude. These were the intimate, unscripted moments that revealed the human side of Hajj, the reflections, and memories that would remain with each pilgrim for life.

At the Jamarat, we documented the determination etched on the faces of those performing the stoning ritual. For many, this act was deeply personal, a tangible way of symbolizing their own battles against temptation and sin. As pilgrims hurled pebbles at the pillars, we captured the power and emotion of the moment, their gestures reflecting both inner struggle and renewed commitment to Allah.

Throughout each day, our team worked tirelessly, editing and crafting these scenes into cohesive stories that could be shared with our audience that very evening. It was a marathon of filming, editing, and broadcasting—capturing not only the rituals but the heartfelt expressions of faith, endurance, and transformation. We hoped that, through these broadcasts, viewers could feel a part of the pilgrimage, touched by the beauty, dedication, and humanity of Hajj.

The final days of Hajj, focused on the remaining ritual of stoning the Jamarat, were relatively straightforward for us. From our position in the media compound, a convenient staircase led directly down to the Jamarat, allowing us to perform the ritual quickly and return within a short time. Compared to the journey faced by many of the hujjaj in the European camps, who often had to walk 45 minutes each way under the intense sun, our experience felt almost effortless. We often heard stories of their perseverance, enduring the heat and long distances to fulfil the ritual, an experience that highlighted their resilience and dedication.

For us, while this Hajj might have seemed easier in some ways, the intense demands of our work layered on their own type of challenge. Filming, editing, and broadcasting day and night, coupled with our commitment to completing all the Hajj rituals, created a rigorous, almost unrelenting schedule. By the end, the cumulative fatigue was undeniable, and despite the easier access to Jamarat, the experience was no less strenuous on our team. The physical demands combined with the spiritual intensity of Hajj made this journey one of both exhaustion and fulfilment, reminding us that every pilgrim faces their own unique test, and ours was a blend of duty and devotion.

On the final day, we wrapped up our last broadcast, marking the end of an intense yet spiritually rewarding experience. With a mix of exhaustion and fulfilment, we began the familiar task of packing up all our equipment, carefully disassembling the cameras, satellite gear, and broadcasting setup that had accompanied us through each stage of Hajj. Once everything was loaded, we made our way back to Makkah for a brief stop, offering our final prayers and bidding farewell to the Ka'bah. With hearts full of gratitude, we then set off to begin the next leg of our journey—to the blessed city of Madinah.

The Madinah segment of our broadcast felt like a profound and much-needed contrast to the intense pace we experienced during Hajj. Here, our workload lightened significantly, allowing us more time to spend in the serene atmosphere of the Prophet's Mosque, Al-Masjid an-Nabawi. Each day, after fulfilling our broadcast duties, we could immerse ourselves in the tranquillity of the Haram, sitting in the Rawdah and offering our prayers in close proximity to the resting place of the Prophet Muhammad (PBUH). This was a deeply spiritual and personal time for each of us, a chance to absorb the blessings of Madinah's peaceful, almost timeless atmosphere.

Our broadcasts focused on exploring the rich history of Madinah, visiting the sites that held immense significance in Islamic history. We filmed at Mount Uhud, where the pivotal battle took place, sharing the story of its martyrs and the lessons from this historic encounter. We visited Masjid Quba, the first mosque built by the Prophet (PBUH), and reflected on the strength and faith that laid its foundation. The sites of

Masjid Qiblatain and the Trench of Khandaq further deepened our appreciation for the sacrifices made by the early Muslims. Each location added layers to our understanding, making us feel like we were not only reporting on history but reconnecting with it in a deeply personal way.

After a week in Madinah, it was time to pack up our equipment for the final time. The reality of leaving hit us as we loaded up for the journey home. Having spent nearly three weeks together in such close quarters, it felt strangely difficult to part ways. The shared experiences of Hajj and Madinah, the moments of exhaustion, the shared meals, and the heartfelt conversations had forged a bond between us that went beyond mere teamwork. We had become brothers, bound by shared spiritual milestones, and leaving behind that unity left a bittersweet feeling.

Over the next ten years, I was blessed to perform six more "working Hajj" journeys, each with a few new team members joining us. Each time, that same spirit of brotherhood reemerged, and each departure brought a renewed sense of emptiness. This team spirit, the camaraderie, and the spiritual bonding left a lasting mark on all of us. These journeys were not just work or worship; they were transformative experiences, carrying memories that would stay with us for a lifetime.

CHAPTER 6

Makkah Twin Peaks

In 2009, I had the immense honour of being invited by the brothers at Ebrahim College to participate in the extraordinary and deeply spiritual initiative known as the Makkah Twin Peaks Challenge. The concept, envisioned by Brother Tufail Hussain, now the UK Director of Islamic Relief, was an inspiring fusion of faith and physical endurance. This ten-day journey was meticulously crafted to combine the sacred acts of Umrah with the physical challenge of climbing two of Islam's most historically significant mountains: Mount Noor and Mount Thawr. More than a pilgrimage, it was a journey of self-discovery, resilience, and reflection, an opportunity to walk in the Prophet Muhammad's (PBUH) footsteps and gain personal insight into the trials and spiritual heights he experienced at these sites.

Guided by knowledgeable scholars, we began in Makkah, preparing ourselves to perform Umrah. Entering the Haram and approaching the Ka'bah was a profoundly moving experience for each of us. As we circled the Ka'bah, we felt the deep resonance of Allah's words in the Qur'an: "And [mention] when We made the House a place of return for the people and a place of security" (Qur'an 2:125). For centuries, this place of refuge, marked by the footsteps of countless prophets, has provided peace and security to millions. In that moment, surrounded by believers from every corner of the world, we felt a profound unity—a bond that transcended language and background, rooted in our shared devotion to Allah. This was a powerful reminder of Islam as a sanctuary, drawing us closer to Allah and connecting us with each other.

After completing Umrah, we braced ourselves for the day's formidable physical challenge: climbing both Mount Noor and Mount Thawr in succession. We began with Mount Noor, known for the Cave of Hira, a place of immense significance, as it was here that the Prophet Muhammad (PBUH) would retreat in solitude to seek closeness to Allah. In this cave, during the final days of Ramadan, he received the first revelation from the angel Jibreel (Gabriel). The path up Mount Noor consists of nearly 1,200 steps, each one demanding as it wound up the mountain's rugged terrain. Our exertion was palpable, but with each step, a sense of anticipation and reverence filled our hearts as we reflected on the Prophet's devotion and his profound moments of contemplation here.

As we neared the summit, Makkah stretched out below us, the Holy Mosque visible in the distance. Standing at the entrance of the Cave of Hira, we were overwhelmed by the significance of the moment. The weight of that first divine command, "Iqra' (Read)" (Qur'an 96:1), washed over us as we considered how these words marked the beginning of a message that would illuminate the world. The small, unassuming cave symbolises the humility and power of Islam's beginnings. Sitting there, we felt a renewed sense of purpose—a reminder of our responsibility to seek knowledge,

live by the teachings of the Qur'an, and carry forward the legacy of the Prophet (PBUH) with sincerity and commitment.

After descending Mount Noor, we prepared for the second climb of the day: Mount Thawr. This mountain, steeped in history and struggle, holds its own unique significance as the place where the Prophet (PBUH) and his closest companion, Abu Bakr (RA), sought refuge in the Cave of Thawr during their flight from Makkah to Madinah. The ascent was challenging, especially after the earlier climb, with sharp inclines and rocky paths that required every ounce of our endurance. But with each step, we were reminded of the Prophet's trials, of the immense trust he placed in Allah, and of the unshakeable strength of faith that sustained both him and Abu Bakr (RA) as they escaped their pursuers. Upon reaching the cave, we paused to reflect on that defining moment when the Prophet (PBUH) reassured Abu Bakr (RA), "Do not be afraid; indeed, Allah is with us" (Qur'an 9:40). Standing there, the weight of that story filled our hearts, and the promise of Allah's protection reminded us of the power of trust and patience in times of hardship.

Through the years, I was blessed to join the Makkah Twin Peaks Challenge multiple times. Each journey offered new insights, deepening my appreciation for these sacred sites and strengthening my connection to the life and sacrifices of the Prophet (PBUH). The trips were often enriched by the presence of esteemed scholars like Sheikh Shams Ad Duha, Sheikh Mujahid Ali, Sheikh Shafi, and Hafidh Mushfique Uddin. Their narrations brought history to life, imbuing each step with meaning. Sheikh Mujahid's retellings of the battles of Uhud and Badr transported us back to those critical moments, while Sheikh Shams Ad Duha's academic approach illuminated the deeper significance behind the rituals. Their guidance added profound layers to our experience, making our climbs and visits to Madinah's historic sites deeply immersive. For many young participants, these experiences were transformative, instilling in them a sense of purpose and devotion. Parents witnessed the changes in their children, recognising the value of this educational and spiritual journey.

One of the most memorable Twin Peaks journeys was in partnership with Al Isharah, an organisation dedicated to supporting the deaf Muslim community. This Umrah journey was unique, as it included a group of brothers and sisters with hearing impairments. Seeing their devotion and enthusiasm brought an entirely new dimension to our pilgrimage. Accompanied by sign language experts proficient in both British and Arabic sign language, these pilgrims engaged fully in every part of Umrah and the climbs, a testament to Islam's inclusivity and universal message. Witnessing their spiritual journey unfold was deeply moving. Allah promises in the Qur'an, "And We certainly have made the Qur'an easy for remembrance" (Qur'an 54:17). This experience brought that verse to life, showing us how Allah's message is accessible to everyone, regardless of their abilities.

The Makkah Twin Peaks Challenge was much more than a physical feat; it was a journey of faith, self-reflection, and connection. Each trip left me with a deeper understanding of the history of Makkah and Madinah, a strengthened appreciation for the sacrifices of the Prophet (PBUH), and a renewed sense of my own commitment to Islam. These experiences planted the seeds for my future work as an Umrah guide, allowing me to share the stories, lessons, and spiritual treasures of these sacred places with others.

Reflecting on these journeys, I recognise how transformative they were, each one a step further in my spiritual growth. They taught me patience, resilience, and the importance of staying connected to the legacy of our beloved Prophet (PBUH). Each climb, each story, and each prayer on these journeys left an indelible mark on my soul, reminding me of the immense privilege of walking, even symbolically, in the footsteps of the Prophet. These memories are treasures, and they continue to inspire me in my journey of faith and service.

CHAPTER 7

Footsteps of the Prophet PBUH

In 2013, while serving as the CEO of Global Aid Trust, I found myself reflecting deeply on the mission and potential impact of our organisation. Global Aid Trust had been founded by a group of prominent scholars, each of whom brought a wealth of knowledge and commitment to our mission. Among these scholars were Ustadh Sheikh Abdur Rahman Madani, Dr. Abul Kalam Azad, Dr. Azadi, and Sheikh Abu Tayyab, all of whom held profound insight into Islamic education and community welfare. Working with these esteemed scholars, I recognised that we had both the resources and expertise to offer something meaningful to our community, beyond immediate aid and support. We had an opportunity to inspire, educate, and shape the next generation.

As I observed the community and its challenges, I became increasingly aware of the need for spiritual and educational programmes that targeted young Muslims. Many were struggling to connect with their heritage and identity, and I could see that a gap existed between the historical richness of Islam and the daily lives of Muslim youth. I realised that we needed an initiative to help bridge this gap, something immersive that would ground them in their history, connect them to the legacy of the Prophet

Muhammad (PBUH), and deepen their faith through experience.

With this in mind, I proposed an ambitious idea to the board: an educational Umrah experience designed specifically for youth. This wouldn't be an ordinary Umrah trip—it would be an intellectually and spiritually enriching journey where participants would explore the life and legacy of the Prophet Muhammad (PBUH) by physically traversing the sacred sites of Makkah and Madinah. We would call it the "Footsteps of the Prophet Muhammad (PBUH) Umrah Project." This project, I envisioned, would not only guide participants through the rituals of Umrah but would take them on a historical and spiritual journey that would make the Seerah come alive.

The aim was to design an experience where every step held purpose, where every site visited became a live classroom. With the support of our board of scholars, I began to shape the programme's itinerary and curriculum, creating a carefully structured journey that would integrate essential teachings with the historical context of each location. Our goal was to provide young Muslims with a transformative experience, not just teaching them the "how" of Umrah, but also the "why" and the "what"—why these sites are so significant, what happened there, and what these events continue to mean for us as Muslims today.

The Umrah trip was crafted to feel like a virtual history class embedded within a pilgrimage. Our journey began with intensive orientation sessions, where participants learned about the significance of Umrah and the importance of understanding the legacy of the Prophet (PBUH) from a historical, spiritual, and personal perspective. Before setting out, each participant was introduced to the key figures of the Seerah—the Prophet Muhammad (PBUH), his family, his companions, and the adversities they faced. We wanted our young participants to see these individuals not just as figures of history, but as real people who had walked these lands and whose courage, patience, and faith laid the foundation of Islam.

As we began the pilgrimage itself, we followed the Prophet's (PBUH) life path, exploring Makkah through the lens of his experiences and sacrifices. Each site we visited became a focal point for reflection and learning. Standing at the Ka'bah, we revisited the story of Ibrahim (AS) and the building of the House of Allah, grounding the youth in the story of faith, dedication, and trust in Allah that began centuries before the Prophet Muhammad (PBUH). With the words from the Qur'an "And [mention] when We made the House a place of return for the people and a place of security" (Qur'an 2:125) resonating in our hearts, we circled the Ka'bah, embodying the unity and timeless connection of our faith.

The journey continued to sites that shaped the Prophet's (PBUH) early life and mission, allowing participants to feel the tangible connection to events they had only read about. Visiting the hills of Safa and Marwah, we reflected on the unwavering faith of Hajar (AS) and the miraculous provision of Zamzam, a well that still sustains millions to this day. Through classes held at each stop, our scholars illuminated the stories behind the rituals, turning each step into a lesson on trust, perseverance, and reliance on Allah.

The most significant part of the journey included a trip to the two mountains, Jabal Noor and Jabal Thawr, each of which played a crucial role in the Prophet's (PBUH) mission. Standing at the base of Jabal Noor, our young participants listened to the story of the Cave of Hira, where the Prophet Muhammad (PBUH) received the first revelation. They learned about his solitude, the weight of the revelation, and the responsibility he accepted to deliver Allah's message to humanity. The climb itself was a test of endurance, mirroring, in a small way, the trials the Prophet (PBUH) endured. Finally reaching the top and standing at the mouth of the cave, the youth were given time to contemplate their own roles as Muslims, to reflect on the words "Iqra" (Read) (Qur'an 96:1), and to recognise their duty to seek knowledge and live by Allah's guidance.

We then took the group to Jabal Thawr, where the Prophet (PBUH) and Abu Bakr (RA) found refuge during their escape to Madinah. The young people learned about the immense faith required as they placed their trust solely in Allah amidst the pursuit of Quraysh. The verse "Do not be afraid; indeed, Allah is with us" (Qur'an 9:40) became more than words; it became a lesson on the resilience and strength of belief. The climb itself was demanding, and as we sat at the cave's entrance, each participant had the chance to connect with the courage of the Prophet (PBUH) and Abu Bakr (RA), understanding that true faith is unwavering, even in the face of adversity.

Our journey continued to Madinah, where the teachings took on a new dimension. We visited the Prophet's Mosque, Badr, and the site of Uhud. Standing at Uhud, the youth heard

about the sacrifices of the companions and learned lessons about the consequences of unity, obedience, and courage. The scholars recounted the Battle of Uhud with such detail that each participant could almost hear the clashing swords and feel the commitment of those who stood with the Prophet (PBUH).

Each session, each site, was designed to make history come alive. The scholars' teachings brought depth and insight to every experience, so that each ritual felt imbued with purpose, every story with relevance. By the end of the journey, the youth returned not only with memories but with a profound understanding of Islam's foundational events, feeling connected to their heritage, identity, and faith in a way that would guide them in the years to come.

The Footsteps of the Prophet Muhammad (PBUH) Umrah Project was more than just a trip; it was an initiation into a lifelong journey of knowledge, reflection, and connection. It was a means of embedding the values of compassion, courage, humility, and faith within the hearts of young Muslims, equipping them to face the world with a resilient sense of identity.

Looking back, this project was a reflection of Global Aid Trust's mission: to serve the immediate needs of the community while empowering the next generation with knowledge and spiritual strength. It was an endeavour that left a lasting impact, both on those who took part and on the organisation itself, setting a high standard for the kind of transformative experiences we aimed to provide for our youth.

Among my most treasured memories of visiting Masjid Nabawi were the deeply impactful lessons I received from Ustadh Sheikh Abdurrahman Madani, who had a unique way of bringing the mosque's historical pillars to life. Ustadh Madani, who had studied at Jamia Madinah and learned under respected scholars such as Sheikh Hudhaifi, would often take my hand, indicating that it was time for a lesson. With each visit, he walked me through Masjid Nabawi, weaving together stories of faith, sacrifice, and love for the Prophet Muhammad (PBUH). These lessons, imparted in the very mosque where the Prophet (PBUH) led his community, left me with an indelible connection to Madinah's sacred heritage.

The Rawdah and the Pillars of Masjid Nabawi

One of the first places Ustadh Madani guided me to was the Rawdah, known as one of the Gardens of Paradise. This area, marked by its distinct green carpet, lies between the Prophet's (PBUH) home and his pulpit, and the Prophet (PBUH) said, "What lies between my house and my pulpit is one of the gardens of Paradise" (Bukhari). Ustadh explained that praying here was akin to being in a piece of Jannah, and I could feel the profound tranquillity enveloping the Rawdah, as though I were in a divine embrace. Here, he introduced me to the pillars of Masjid Nabawi, each with its own story, each a silent witness to pivotal moments in early Islamic history.

Ustuwanah al-Hannanah (The Pillar of the Weeping Date Palm)

We began with Ustuwanah al-Hannanah, also known as the "Pillar of the Weeping Date Palm." Ustadh recounted the beautiful story behind this pillar. Originally, the Prophet (PBUH) would lean against a date palm trunk when giving his sermons. However, when a new pulpit was built for him, he began using it instead. As soon as he left the date palm, it began to cry out, yearning for the Prophet's (PBUH) presence. In response, the Prophet (PBUH) embraced the trunk until it stopped weeping, comforting it like a beloved friend. This story moved me deeply; Ustadh explained that even an inanimate object felt the absence of the Prophet (PBUH), teaching us about the profound love that radiated from him. The date palm's yearning was a reminder of the attachment and love we too should have for the Messenger (PBUH).

Ustuwanah al-Sarir (The Pillar of the Prophet's Bed)

Next, Ustadh led me to Ustuwanah al-Sarir, or "The Pillar of the Prophet's Bed." This pillar marks the place where the Prophet (PBUH) would sometimes spend the night in worship, away from his family's quarters. Ustadh explained how the Prophet (PBUH) would lay his mat here, worshipping until dawn in deep connection with Allah. This pillar became a reminder of the Prophet's devotion, his nights spent in prayer and supplication for his Ummah, his selflessness, and his enduring dedication to Allah. Standing before it, I was humbled, reminded of the importance of private worship, and the spiritual strength the Prophet (PBUH) gained from it.

Ustuwanah al-Tawbah (The Pillar of Repentance)

We then visited Ustuwanah al-Tawbah, or "The Pillar of Repentance," also known as the "Pillar of Abu Lubabah." Ustadh Madani recounted the story of Abu Lubabah (RA), a companion who, after feeling deep remorse for a mistake, tied himself to this pillar, vowing not to leave until Allah forgave him. The Prophet (PBUH) brought him the glad tidings of forgiveness, releasing him from his vow. Ustadh explained that this pillar symbolises the boundless mercy of

Allah and the power of sincere repentance. He reminded me that no sin is too great to be forgiven when repentance is genuine, as exemplified by Abu Lubabah's story.

Ustuwanah al-Haras (The Pillar of the Guard)

The next stop was Ustuwanah al-Haras, or "The Pillar of the Guard," where Ali ibn Abi Talib (RA) and others would stand guard to protect the Prophet (PBUH). In the early days, there was a real threat to the Prophet's (PBUH) life, and his companions took turns keeping watch over him as he slept nearby. This pillar symbolised the dedication and loyalty of the Prophet's (PBUH) companions, who were willing to sacrifice everything to safeguard him and the message of Islam. Ustadh spoke of how Ali (RA) would stay awake, protecting the Prophet (PBUH), his loyalty unwavering. This pillar became a symbol of true brotherhood and selflessness, qualities we should strive to embody.

Ustuwanah al-Wufud (The Pillar of Delegations)

We then moved to Ustuwanah al-Wufud, or "The Pillar of Delegations." Ustadh explained that this was the place where delegations from various tribes would come to meet the Prophet (PBUH) and embrace Islam. Here, he welcomed dignitaries, ambassadors, and tribes, inviting them to understand Islam and witness his noble character firsthand. Ustadh shared how the Prophet's (PBUH) humility and wisdom had won the hearts of people from diverse backgrounds, drawing them to Islam. This pillar symbolises the spread of Islam and the Prophet's (PBUH) role as a leader who showed patience, diplomacy, and kindness to those who sought his counsel.

Ustuwanah al-Muhajirin (The Pillar of the Emigrants)

We reached Ustuwanah al-Muhajirin, or "The Pillar of the Emigrants." This pillar was where the Prophet (PBUH) would meet the early Muslims who had emigrated from Makkah, those who had left their homes and families behind for the sake of Allah. Ustadh Madani spoke of the sacrifices made by the Muhajirin, who endured immense hardship but remained steadfast in their devotion. This pillar symbolises sacrifice, patience, and unwavering faith. Standing here, I reflected on the courage and resilience of these early Muslims, realising that their sacrifices allowed Islam to flourish and reach us today.

The Mihrab of the Prophet (PBUH)

One of the most significant places Ustadh took me to was the Mihrab of the Prophet (PBUH), where he would lead his community in prayer. The mihrab marks the direction of prayer and is a symbol of unity, as Muslims worldwide turn to this same qibla. Ustadh explained that leading prayer was a weighty responsibility, one the Prophet (PBUH) fulfilled with humility and devotion. In this place, he not only led

prayers but also strengthened the bonds of the early community, fostering a spirit of compassion, brotherhood, and solidarity. Standing before the mihrab, I felt the timeless unity of the Ummah, a bond that reaches across geography and generations.

The Pulpit of the Prophet (PBUH)

Finally, we stood before the Mimbar (Pulpit), where the Prophet (PBUH) delivered sermons to his companions. Ustadh shared stories of the powerful sermons delivered here, especially the famous Farewell Sermon, where the Prophet (PBUH) outlined principles of equality, justice, and respect that remain timeless. He reminded me of the power of words to inspire change and the importance of conveying wisdom with humility. This pulpit symbolised the Prophet's

(PBUH) role as a teacher and leader, guiding his community with compassion and strength.

The Hidden Pool at Uhud

In addition to these pillars, there was one other location that held special meaning—a hidden spot at the site of the Battle of Uhud. One day, Ustadh Madani took my hand and led me away from the main group to a secluded area across the road from the Mountain of Archers. Tucked within the crevices of the mountain was a small, almost hidden pool of water. Ustadh explained that this was where the Prophet's (PBUH) daughter, Fatimah (RA), brought him to wash his wounds after he was gravely injured during the battle. This private and unassuming spot held a poignant story of love, resilience, and sacrifice, hidden from most visitors but deeply significant to those who knew it. In this quiet place, I could feel the weight of the hardships the Prophet (PBUH) endured for his mission, and the immense love his family had for him.

The house of Ayub Al Ansari (RA)

One of the most unforgettable lessons I received from Ustadh Sheikh Abdurrahman Madani was about the story of Abu Ayyub Al-Ansari (RA) and his house, a place that holds profound significance in the history of Islam. This lesson took place just outside Masjid Nabawi, as we walked through the streets of Madinah. As he often did, Ustadh Madani grasped my hand, signalling that he was about to impart a lesson close to his heart. His voice took on a reverent tone as he guided me to the spot where, centuries ago, the house of Abu Ayyub Al-Ansari (RA) once stood.

Abu Ayyub Al-Ansari (RA) was one of the early Ansar—those residents of Madinah who welcomed the Prophet Muhammad (PBUH) and the emigrants (Muhajirun) from Makkah. His deep love for the Prophet (PBUH) and unwavering faith had already distinguished him as a beloved member of the community. When the Prophet Muhammad (PBUH) made his migration from Makkah to Madinah, it was Abu Ayyub who had the honour of hosting him, a privilege and responsibility he embraced with his entire heart.

Ustadh Madani began by painting the scene of the Prophet's arrival in Madinah. After a long and arduous journey, the Prophet (PBUH) entered Madinah to an enthusiastic and joyful welcome from its residents, who were eager to host him. Families stood in anticipation, hoping that the Prophet (PBUH) would choose to stay with them. The joy of Madinah's people was boundless, each person and tribe yearning for the blessing of hosting Allah's Messenger. But the Prophet (PBUH), with characteristic wisdom and humility, allowed his camel, Qaswa, to choose the spot where he would stay, saying, "Leave her, for she is under command."

As the people of Madinah eagerly watched, Qaswa trotted through the streets until she stopped in front of the humble house of Abu Ayyub Al-Ansari (RA). This was a man of modest means, but his heart overflowed with faith and love for the Prophet (PBUH). Abu Ayyub (RA) was overjoyed, seeing in this seemingly random choice the hand of divine guidance.

The Prophet (PBUH) accepted Abu Ayyub's invitation with graciousness and humility, making this home his residence until the construction of Masjid Nabawi and the adjoining quarters for the Prophet's family could be completed.

Ustadh Madani continued, recounting how Abu Ayyub Al-Ansari (RA) and his family adjusted their lives to accommodate the Prophet (PBUH). Abu Ayyub's house was simple, with only two levels. Out of respect, he and his wife took the upper floor, offering the lower floor to the Prophet (PBUH) for convenience and privacy. However, as night fell, Abu Ayyub (RA) became deeply troubled. He and his wife could not bear the thought of sleeping above the Prophet (PBUH), fearing it would be disrespectful to have their feet positioned over him. That night, they moved to a corner of the upper floor, trying not to make a sound so as not to disturb him. Ustadh described how Abu Ayyub's (RA) heart was filled with a blend of humility, awe, and profound respect for the Prophet (PBUH), emotions that kept him restless throughout the night.

The next morning, Abu Ayyub (RA) approached the Prophet (PBUH) with a humble request, asking him to take the upper floor while he and his wife would move downstairs. The Prophet (PBUH), always sensitive to others' feelings, agreed to Abu Ayyub's request, understanding the respect and devotion that prompted it. Ustadh Madani explained that this small but profound act revealed the deep love the Ansar had for the Prophet (PBUH) and the lengths they would go to honour him.

As the days passed, Abu Ayyub (RA) continued to serve the Prophet (PBUH) with unmatched devotion. Ustadh Madani shared a touching story of one evening when Abu Ayyub (RA) prepared a meal for the Prophet (PBUH). He brought the food downstairs, placing it gently before him. After the Prophet (PBUH) had finished, Abu Ayyub eagerly retrieved the plate, seeking the places where the Prophet's (PBUH) blessed hands had touched the food. He and his wife would eat from those specific parts, hoping to absorb the barakah (blessing) of the Prophet (PBUH).

Ustadh Madani paused here, letting the beauty of Abu Ayyub's (RA) love and reverence sink in. He explained that Abu Ayyub's devotion wasn't about formality or tradition; it was about genuine love and a desire to be close to the Prophet (PBUH) in every way possible. Abu Ayyub (RA) saw in the Prophet (PBUH) the embodiment of all that was beautiful and righteous, and he yearned to be near him, not just physically, but spiritually.

Ustadh also recounted a story that showed the Prophet's (PBUH) sensitivity and kindness towards Abu Ayyub (RA). One night, a small jug of water accidentally spilled on the upper floor where Abu Ayyub (RA) and his wife slept. Fearful that even a drop might drip onto the Prophet (PBUH) below, they hurriedly used their only blanket to soak up the water, leaving themselves without any cover for the night. Their selflessness and concern were purely out of love for the Messenger of Allah (PBUH), a sentiment that profoundly touched everyone who knew them.

Ustadh Madani explained that the Prophet's (PBUH) stay in Abu Ayyub's house was no mere accident—it was a testament to the bond between the Prophet (PBUH) and the Ansar, who would go on to support him and the message of Islam with their lives and wealth. Abu Ayyub's (RA) house became a centre of faith, a sanctuary where the Prophet (PBUH) could find peace amid the challenges of his mission. His residence there symbolised the generosity and hospitality that the people of Madinah offered to the Muhajirun, creating a model of community support and mutual respect that would characterise the Muslim community.

As Ustadh finished the story, he squeezed my hand, a reminder to hold onto these lessons with all my heart. The spot where we stood, near the site of Abu Ayyub's house, was no longer marked by a building, yet its significance resonated deeply. Through this story, I understood the profound devotion the early Muslims had for the Prophet (PBUH). It wasn't about titles or grand gestures; it was about a simple, heartfelt love that expressed itself in acts of respect, humility, and selflessness.

Reflecting on the story of Abu Ayyub (RA), I realised that his example was a reminder of how to honour the legacy of the Prophet (PBUH) today—not just in grand displays of worship, but in genuine love, humility, and service. This lesson from Ustadh Madani stays with me as a guiding light, a model of the kind of heart I aspire to cultivate. Every visit to Madinah reminds me of the love and dedication of Abu Ayyub (RA), a devotion so sincere that it continues to inspire hearts centuries later.

Through these lessons, Ustadh Madani helped me see that Masjid Nabawi and the sites of Madinah were more than historic places; they were living symbols of faith, devotion, and love. Each pillar and each place represented a story, a lesson, and a legacy left by the Prophet (PBUH) and his companions. Ustadh's gentle grip on my hand was more than a gesture; it was a reminder to absorb these lessons deeply, to carry them within my heart, and to live by them. His teachings brought Madinah to life for me, making these sites an enduring source of inspiration and guidance.

The lessons on Taif and Masjid Ad Das

The story of Taif and Masjid Ad-Das holds a profound place in the Seerah of the Prophet Muhammad (PBUH), yet, like many, I only truly understood its depth when I experienced it firsthand. Throughout my childhood, I'd heard about the Prophet's journey to Taif—the mistreatment he endured, the stones that rained upon him, and the physical and emotional suffering he bore with patience. But it was only years later, standing in Masjid Ad-Das with Ustadh by my side, that the story truly came alive.

One day, as he had done many times before, Ustadh took me by the hand and led me to this modest, unassuming mosque, Masjid Ad-Das.

Here, as we stood quietly, he began to recount the story of Taif. In the 10th year of prophethood, after the passing of his beloved wife Khadijah (RA) and his supportive uncle Abu Talib, the Prophet (PBUH) faced mounting opposition in Makkah. Seeking a new audience for the message of Islam, he set out on foot to Taif, a town nestled among the mountains and known for its fertile land and influential tribes.

Arriving in Taif, he approached the leaders of the town, hoping to find those who might listen with open hearts. But rather than welcoming him, they met him with hostility, mockery, and rejection. The leaders not only turned him away but incited the town's youth and servants to follow him out of the city, hurling stones at him. With no refuge, the Prophet (PBUH) was left bruised and bleeding, his sandals filling with his own blood as he struggled to protect himself from the barrage of stones.

In Masjid Ad-Das, Ustadh paused to let the weight of this story settle in. I could feel the gravity of what it must have been like for the Prophet (PBUH), standing alone, hurt, humiliated, and cast out by those he wished only to guide. But amidst the sorrow of that day, a moment of mercy emerged, one that transformed the story from one of rejection to one of hope.

In his exhausted state, the Prophet (PBUH) took refuge in a small vineyard. The vineyard was owned by Utbah and Shaybah, wealthy men of Quraysh who had set it aside as a

retreat. Seeing the Prophet's condition, they sent a Christian servant, Ad-Das, with a tray of grapes to offer him some relief. When Ad-Das approached, the Prophet (PBUH) graciously accepted the grapes, beginning with the words, "Bismillah" (In the name of Allah). This simple phrase struck Ad-Das, who had never heard it spoken in Taif. Curious, Ad-Das asked the Prophet (PBUH) where he was from, and upon learning that the Prophet (PBUH) was from Makkah, he mentioned that he was from Nineveh, the city of Yunus (Jonah). Smiling, the Prophet (PBUH) shared with Ad-Das that he, too, was a prophet, like Yunus. Overcome with awe, Ad-Das leaned down, kissed the Prophet's hands and feet, and declared his faith, recognising the truth in the Prophet's message.

As Ustadh shared this story in Masjid Ad-Das, he made me understand that this moment with Ad-Das was more than an act of kindness; it was a reminder of Allah's mercy, even in the Prophet's darkest moments. Despite the cruelty of Taif's people, Allah sent solace through a single soul who saw the light of Islam. It was as if Allah was telling His beloved Messenger (PBUH) that, even in hardship, his mission was still valuable, and there were hearts ready to be guided.

Standing in Masjid Ad-Das, with Ustadh's words bringing the scene to life, I could almost feel the presence of the Prophet (PBUH) in that vineyard, his unyielding resilience, and the strength of his trust in Allah. The story of Taif was no longer just a story I'd heard as a child; it was a reminder of the Prophet's (PBUH) profound compassion, his commitment to his mission, and the ways Allah's mercy manifests even in the harshest trials. This experience, taught in the very place where Ad-Das encountered the Prophet (PBUH), is one that remains close to my heart. The memory serves as a reminder that no matter how challenging life becomes, we must persevere with faith, as our hardships may be the very pathways through which Allah's mercy and wisdom reach us.

One of the greatest insights I carry from these trips and the lessons with Ustadh Madani is that no matter how many books one reads, the experience of being taught by a knowledgeable scholar while standing in these sacred, historical locations is unmatched. Books can provide knowledge, but often we read without truly absorbing the information or feeling the spirit of the words. Learning directly from Ustadh at the very sites where Islamic history unfolded left an imprint on my heart and mind that no book alone could have achieved. These lessons are etched deeply within me, and they resonate in the work I do today as an Umrah guide.

Photo by Jumanh Jammaz on Unsplash (https://unsplash.com/@jmnlh)

CHAPTER 8
The Umrah of Mourning & Glad Tidings

Whenever I've faced difficult moments in life—and there have been many—my 'go-to' place has always been Makkah and Madinah. For me, and for countless others, these sacred cities are not just destinations; they are sanctuaries of the soul. They are where you feel closest to Allah, where your heart unburdens its heaviest sorrows, and where a profound sense of peace envelops you. There, amid the echoes of faith and the serenity of prayer, one finds clarity, strength, and the gentle reminder that Allah's mercy is infinite.

In 2022, we were looking forward to what we believed would be a joyous chapter in our family's story. My wife was expecting our second child, and we were overjoyed. Our eldest son, Zayn, was only 9 months old, and the thought of him having a baby brother to grow up with filled us with happiness. We had already chosen a name—Raiyyan. We pictured him in our arms, completing our little family. But life, as it so often does, had different plans.

As the delivery approached, complications began to surface. What should have been a time of anticipation turned into days of uncertainty and quiet prayers. The doctors confirmed that the pregnancy was at risk, and my wife was admitted to the hospital. For 10 long days, we held onto hope, each moment a delicate balance between faith and fear. Zayn, still a baby himself, needed his mother, but the hospital's restrictions often kept him away. It was a time of immense emotional strain—juggling Zayn's needs, supporting my wife, and bracing ourselves for what Allah had decreed.

On the 10th day, despite the tireless efforts of the medical staff, our second son passed away shortly after birth. The weight of that loss is something I struggle to put into words. My wife was still unconscious, and I was left to bear the grief alone, if only for a while. When she awoke, I faced the unbearable task of telling her. Yet, her response humbled me in ways I will never forget. She smiled softly, her faith shining through her tears, and said, *"Look how fortunate we are. We have one child with us, and another who awaits us in Jannah."* Her strength in that moment was extraordinary—a testament to her unwavering trust in Allah's wisdom. She became my anchor when I felt adrift in sorrow.

A week after returning home, I led the janazah of my own son and buried him with my own hands. The weight of holding his tiny body, lowering him into the earth, and whispering prayers over him is a memory that will never leave me. Yet, even in that heartbreak, there was a strange solace in knowing that he was in the care of Allah, untouched by the trials of this world.

In the days that followed, grief lingered heavily, but I realized that both my wife and I needed healing. Seeking solace, I booked tickets for our first Umrah as a family. With Zayn, just 10 months old, we travelled to Makkah and Madinah immediately after Ramadan. That journey became a turning point—*a mourning and healing Umrah* that brought us closer together and closer to Allah.

I still remember carrying Zayn in a baby carrier during tawaf, my wife walking beside me. In the presence of the Ka'bah, surrounded by the tranquillity of Makkah, I felt an indescribable peace. The sadness that had weighed us down began to lift with every step, every prayer. It was as if the sacred spaces absorbed our pain and replaced it with a quiet strength. We returned home, not just as a family, but as a stronger, more united family.

Months later, I gifted an Umrah package to my eldest niece and her husband as a wedding present. Around the same time, my wife mentioned a dream in which she saw the Ka'bah. Taking it as a sign, I planned another Umrah for our anniversary. During that visit, while in Madinah, we received glad tidings of another blessing to come. Our son Deen was born the following June—a beautiful reminder of Allah's mercy and the cycle of loss and renewal.

Alhamdulillah, as I write this, Zayn, now 3 years and 4 months old, has completed five Umrah trips. Deen, just 1 year and 5 months, has already been blessed with three trips to the sacred cities. Watching them grow and experience the beauty of Makkah and Madinah has been a joy beyond words.

Traveling with young children to these sacred places often feels daunting for many parents, but from my experience, it is more manageable than it seems—especially when they are infants. On our first trip with Zayn, we made small adjustments, like buying a walker in Taif for him to use at the hotel, which made our stay much easier. Over time, we became more prepared for the challenges, from navigating baby food options to keeping up with a crawling or walking toddler. By our third trip, managing both Zayn and Deen came with its share of activity, but even amidst the busyness, moments like watching Zayn crawl on the green carpets of Masjid Nabawi or seeing both boys light up in the vast open courtyards were unforgettable.

On our most recent Umrah, with Zayn as a lively toddler and Deen just learning to walk, there were moments of chaos. But the beauty of Makkah and Madinah is that no matter the time of day or night, the cities are safe, serene, and welcoming. The boys loved the freedom of being outdoors, surrounded by the sacred atmosphere.

For parents considering Umrah with young children, my advice is simple: embrace it. Yes, it takes preparation and patience, but the rewards far outweigh the challenges. These moments in the sacred cities, shared as a family, are blessings that will stay with you forever.

My hope, InshaAllah, is to continue taking my sons to Makkah and Madinah at least once a year. I want them to grow up with a connection to these sacred cities so profound that it shapes their character and remains a source of guidance and strength throughout their lives. I pray that their bond with Makkah and Madinah stays with them, anchoring their hearts in faith and reminding them of Allah's mercy as they navigate the journey of life.

Photo by said alamri on Unsplash (https://unsplash.com/@saidalamri63)

CHAPTER 9

Umrah Guide

Looking back, it's clear that becoming an Umrah guide was never part of my plans or even within the realm of my ambitions. I remember an encounter after my second Umrah that, in hindsight, was perhaps a subtle nudge in this direction. I was at an event, perhaps a mosque gathering, when I struck up a conversation with a gentleman who, as we talked, handed me his business card. On it was written "Khadimul Hujjaj" – "Servant of the Pilgrims." Seeing those words moved me in a way I couldn't quite explain. I looked at him with newfound admiration, thinking, Imagine the honour it must be to serve the Hujjaj, to facilitate their journeys to the holiest places on earth. That sense of awe stayed with me, but I could never have imagined that one day I would be fortunate enough to carry out that role myself.

Years later, even after I had completed over thirty trips to Makkah and Madinah, I still did not consider myself equipped to guide others on such a spiritually profound journey. Being an Umrah guide requires more than just logistical knowledge; it demands a depth of understanding that is authentic, well-researched, and above all, rooted in genuine reverence for the rituals and the sacred history they encapsulate. I had been on various Umrah excursions where, regrettably, I witnessed some guides embellishing or dramatising the sacred stories, often to evoke a strong emotional reaction from the group. I could see why they did it; the more evocative the narrative, the more likely it was that pilgrims would respond generously with a hadiya (a gift in kind) at the end. But this approach left me disheartened.

Why alter or embellish something so sacred? The authentic accounts of the Prophet's (PBUH) life, the stories of the Companions, and the significance of each site carry an inherent beauty and emotional power that doesn't need embellishment. I felt a growing responsibility to honour these truths without theatrics, to communicate the essence of these holy places in a way that would leave a lasting impact on the pilgrims' hearts based on authenticity alone.

It was this commitment to truth, coupled with the experiences and lessons I'd gained over the years, that finally drew me into the role of an Umrah guide. I now see every pilgrimage I guide as an opportunity to impart what I have learned, just as my Ustadh did for me. I hope that, by Allah's mercy, this work may serve as a form of sadaqa jariya (continuous charity) for my Ustadh, and perhaps even for myself, if Allah accepts it. To be able to serve pilgrims, guiding them to the Ka'bah and the Prophet's (PBUH) mosque, is truly an honour beyond words—one I could once only dream of and one that still humbles me with every journey.

I didn't actually begin taking on the role of an Umrah guide until I had completed at least 40 Umrah trips. I had set myself on a mission: to learn thoroughly, to verify meticulously, and to seek authentic evidence from reliable, primary sources. As a trained lawyer, I approached this endeavour with a deep sense of responsibility. For me, it wasn't simply about knowing the stories or recounting them emotionally; it was about ensuring that every detail I shared was anchored in solid, verifiable sources. Islam places a high emphasis on knowledge, but even more so on the responsibility to disperse that knowledge accurately. The Prophet Muhammad (PBUH) famously said, "Convey from me, even if it is only one verse" (Bukhari). This is a call to share knowledge, but also a reminder to ensure that what we convey is truthful, precise, and faithfully represents the essence of Islam.

My starting point on this journey of preparation was to revisit the Seerah of the Prophet (PBUH). I began with "Ar-Raheeq Al-Makhtoum" (The Sealed Nectar), a well-known text that provides a structured overview of the Prophet's life. However, I soon realised that while the book is invaluable, it offers a more summarised version of events, which only scratched the surface of the depth I wanted to reach. As someone who had taken on this responsibility, I felt compelled to seek a more detailed and nuanced understanding. I began searching for a comprehensive course or lecture series that could delve into the intricacies of the Seerah, providing context and depth that I could share with future pilgrims.

After much searching, I turned to a lecture series by my close friend and respected Ustadh, Sheikh Shady Al-Suleiman, a Palestinian scholar residing in Australia. Sheikh Shady's dedication to knowledge and dawah work was well known. We had met on numerous occasions at various events, and during one of my 'working Hajj' trips, he accompanied me on several broadcasts. I also had the privilege of visiting his expansive dawah centre in Melbourne, where he continues to educate and inspire Muslims from all walks of life.

Sheikh Shady's Seerah series, available on YouTube, spans approximately 100 hours, covering the life of the Prophet (PBUH) with incredible detail and insight. This series offered the depth and context I had been searching for. For hours on end, I dedicated myself to not just watching these lectures but taking extensive notes, re-reading specific passages, and cross-referencing with other sources to ensure consistency. This study wasn't passive; it was an active effort to immerse myself in the life of the Prophet (PBUH), to understand not only the sequence of events but the lessons, wisdom, and nuances embedded within each story.

Even then, I sometimes found myself grappling with certain areas where I wanted additional perspective or clarity. In those moments, I would reach out to my beloved Ustadh, Sheikh Abdurrahman Madani, who has an unparalleled depth of knowledge, particularly on the finer points of Islamic history. Consulting Ustadh Madani became a vital part of my process, helping me refine my understanding and approach to certain topics. His insights, steeped in both academic rigour and lived experience, provided me with invaluable guidance, reinforcing my commitment to maintaining accuracy and authenticity.

Becoming an Umrah guide is no light responsibility. It's a role that requires not just knowledge but the humility to continually seek clarity and to ensure that the information shared is of the highest integrity. I realised that I was not just guiding people through the physical locations; I was guiding them through the emotional, spiritual, and intellectual journey of the Prophet's life. Pilgrims deserved to receive knowledge that was authentic and unembellished knowledge that would deepen their connection to their faith and to the legacy of the Prophet (PBUH).

To this day, I approach my role as an Umrah guide with the same dedication. I strive to ensure that every story, every detail, is relayed with accuracy, sincerity, and respect for the sacred history we are privileged to recount. My journey in becoming an Umrah guide has become an ongoing process of learning, verifying, and humbly conveying the truth. And in doing so, I hope that my work can serve as a form of sadaqa jariya—a continuous charity for those who taught me, especially Ustadh Madani and Sheikh Shady, if Allah wills to accept it. Their guidance, wisdom, and commitment to the faith continue to inspire me, and it is my prayer that every lesson shared will leave a lasting impact on those who embark on this blessed journey.

Another challenge I faced in my journey as an Umrah guide was delivering this knowledge in two languages—English and Bangla. Growing up in the UK since infancy, my command of Bangla was basic at best. My fluency was limited to casual conversations, mostly with my parents, where I could express myself but lacked depth and formality. Then, around 20 years ago, I found myself drawn into presenting on Bangla-language television channels, even though my Bangla at that time was far from polished. It was an emergency situation, and the only option was to adapt quickly. I spent nearly a year in intensive self-study, working hard to improve my pronunciation, grammar, and overall language skills to a level deemed suitable for television.

This period required dedication and rapid learning. I spent countless hours watching Bangla TV programmes, listening to how presenters spoke with clarity and precision, and reading Bangla newspapers to familiarise myself with formal vocabulary and sentence structure. Bit by bit, I started refining my pronunciation and expanding my vocabulary, and while it was challenging, it paid off. Over time, my confidence grew, and I was able to present more comfortably in Bangla. Even today, it surprises me when people compliment my Bangla, saying, "Your Bangla is really good." The truth, however, is that my vocabulary remains limited. What I do have is an emphasis on clear pronunciation and careful speech, which can sometimes create the impression of fluency.

When I guide an Umrah group, this language divide becomes even more pronounced. Delivering my talks in English is quite straightforward—I can speak with confidence, choosing words that are expressive and nuanced, given my strong command of the language. However, when translating that same content into Bangla, I encounter significant limitations. Many of the nuanced terms and ideas I am comfortable with in English simply don't exist in my Bangla vocabulary, and I struggle to find the words that would capture their full meaning. For example, in the context of the Seerah, words related to historical events, theological principles, or the subtleties of certain stories have specific connotations that can be challenging to convey accurately in Bangla.

In fact, if one were to listen to me deliver the same seminar in both languages, they would immediately notice that the Bangla version is much simpler. In Bangla, I rely on more straightforward terms and use a limited vocabulary to express ideas that I could explain more effectively in English. Often, I feel that there's more I could convey in Bangla if I had the words. I've learned to simplify my explanations, yet I sometimes worry that this simplicity may miss some of the nuances and depth that these stories and lessons deserve.

This challenge has motivated me to keep working on my Bangla, both in vocabulary and depth of expression. I have a long way to go, but I am committed to improving, knowing that a refined ability to convey these teachings in Bangla would allow me to reach a wider audience, especially those who may feel more connected to the language of their heritage. My hope is that, over time, I'll be able to bridge this gap and deliver in Bangla with the same clarity, detail, and reverence I can achieve in English. Until then, I continue striving, knowing that each attempt, however imperfect, is part of my own journey of growth in serving Allah's message.

So far, I have had the privilege of guiding just over 20 individual Umrah trips, working with various groups and providers. Each group has brought with it a diverse range of participants, each with unique perspectives, motivations, and expectations for their journey. My experiences with these groups have been enlightening, as I've encountered people spanning the full spectrum—from those who come with an intense eagerness to learn and absorb as much as possible, to those who prefer a more independent experience, immersing themselves in personal worship and reflection.

With this diversity in mind, I've found it essential to approach the educational aspect of the Umrah journey thoughtfully. Over time, I've developed a flexible style that seeks to balance structured learning with the personal space each pilgrim needs. Rather than setting rigid times for seminars or educational sessions, I adapt the learning component to natural gathering points—times when the group is already assembled, such as during bus journeys between sacred sites or while waiting together at a particular location. This approach has proven effective, as it creates an environment where people can listen, reflect, and discuss without feeling that their personal worship time is being compromised.

For example, when travelling between Makkah and Madinah, I often use the travel time to discuss the historical and spiritual significance of each city, recounting key events in the Seerah and drawing connections to the sites we'll visit. This creates a seamless integration of learning within the journey itself, allowing participants to engage with the historical context without having to set aside extra time outside their planned ibadah.

On a few occasions, I've experimented with holding additional, optional seminars at separate times, such as in the hotel conference room or at quieter times in the masjid courtyard. However, the turnout for these sessions has often been limited, not necessarily due to a lack of interest, but because many pilgrims arrive with specific spiritual goals and schedules. Being in Makkah and Madinah is a deeply personal experience for many, and people naturally want to maximise their time in prayer, tawaf, and other acts of worship. I respect this immensely; after all, these are the heart of the journey. So, I've learned to remain sensitive to each pilgrim's needs, finding a balance that supports both communal learning and individual devotion.

In some groups, there are participants who crave more depth and ask questions that spark longer discussions—often leading us to touch on topics beyond the usual itinerary. I relish these moments, as they bring forth a richer, more interactive experience, where both the questions and reflections of participants bring added meaning to the journey. For instance, a question about the life of the Prophet (PBUH) or the stories of his companions can transform a brief teaching moment into a deeply engaging discussion, and these spontaneous exchanges often become the highlights of the trip.

Ultimately, guiding an Umrah journey is about finding harmony between structured guidance and the individual experience each pilgrim seeks. My aim is to make the journey both enriching and flexible, allowing people to connect to their faith in a way that feels personal yet grounded in shared understanding. Over time, I've come to see each group as a unique gathering with its own dynamics, where learning is woven into the journey itself rather than confined to set times. And, in doing so, I hope to provide an Umrah experience that is not only educational but also respectful of each pilgrim's spiritual aspirations.

In concluding this chapter, I feel it's essential to reflect on my personal motivation for doing this work and guiding these journeys. Guiding an Umrah pilgrimage is not just about accompanying people to Makkah and Madinah; it's about helping them find meaning and purpose in the experience and connecting them to a deeper understanding of their faith. My last short lecture, typically delivered on the coach as we head to the airport for our return to the UK, focuses on a vital question: What is our takeaway from this journey? What are we truly bringing back with us?

I often emphasise that our 'takeaway' should be more than the tangible items—like dates, zamzam, or souvenirs—that we carry back to our loved ones. While these are meaningful symbols of our journey, they are not the essence of what we should strive to bring home. The real takeaway lies in something much deeper: a renewed commitment to grow in our deen and a thirst to seek knowledge.

This emphasis on learning and personal growth aligns with the very first command Allah revealed to the Prophet Muhammad (PBUH): "Iqra'" (Read) (Qur'an 96:1). This command signifies the foundation of our faith—one that begins with knowledge and understanding. The Prophet

(PBUH) also underscored this, teaching us that "Seeking knowledge is an obligation upon every Muslim" (Ibn Majah). This journey is not just a religious obligation but an ongoing spiritual duty that should inspire us to seek knowledge and better ourselves throughout our lives.

In this final reflection, I stress three key takeaways that, if held onto, can transform this journey into a lasting change:

1. **Discipline in Worship** – Over the course of our pilgrimage, we've engaged in a form of intensive training (tarbiyah) that has conditioned us to prioritise prayer, to hasten to the masjid for salah, and to value punctuality in our acts of worship. The Holy Qur'an reminds us, "Verily, the prayer is enjoined on the believers at fixed hours" (Qur'an 4:103). Our pilgrimage has reinforced this discipline, reminding us of the importance of praying on time and cultivating a connection to the masjid. If we can take this discipline back with us, making it part of our daily routine, we carry the spirit of Umrah into our lives.
2. **Mindfulness of Behaviour and Speech** – In the sacred lands, we've been exceptionally conscious of our words, our actions, and our interactions with others, striving to embody kindness, patience, and humility. The Prophet (PBUH) taught us, "Whoever believes in Allah and the Last Day should speak a good word or remain silent" (Bukhari and Muslim). This pilgrimage has heightened our awareness of our behaviour, reminding us to carry this same mindfulness into our daily lives. If we can maintain this vigilance over our actions and speech, we are embracing a key aspect of our faith.

3. **Attachment to the Qur'an** – During this journey, we have developed a renewed bond with the Qur'an, reciting it more frequently, reflecting on its verses, and feeling its guidance more intimately. The Prophet (PBUH) said, "The best of you are those who learn the Qur'an and teach it" (Bukhari). If we can carry this attachment home, making time for the Qur'an in our daily lives, we not only nurture our own connection to Allah but inspire those around us as well. Our hearts, softened by the words of Allah, are in the best state to absorb its lessons.

In essence, if we return with these three takeaways—a commitment to disciplined worship, a mindful approach to our behaviour, and a strong attachment to the Qur'an—then we have truly gained the best treasure, or 'ghanimah,' from this journey. This 'treasure' is priceless, a legacy from the holy lands that can shape our lives for the better and bring us closer to Allah. As we return home, I pray that these takeaways stay with us, growing and guiding us long after the pilgrimage has ended, turning this journey into a lasting chapter of spiritual growth.

CHAPTER 10

The Basics of Umrah

If you're preparing to embark on Umrah this year, know that this is more than just a journey—it's a calling. Allah has invited you to His house, and that's no small privilege. Out of countless people, He has chosen you to stand before the Ka'bah, to feel the unity of the Ummah, and to experience the peace and renewal that comes with being in the sacred lands. Take a moment to appreciate this invitation deeply, with humility and gratitude, for it's a chance not everyone receives. Thank Allah for granting you this opportunity, for giving you the means and the health to travel. He has drawn you near, and that's a blessing beyond measure.

With this incredible opportunity before you, it's important to make the most of it. Approaching Umrah with sincerity and understanding will help you absorb its rewards and deepen your connection with Allah. Umrah is not just a series of rituals—it's a journey of transformation, and to fully experience its impact, we need to approach each step with knowledge and reverence.

To guide you, let's walk through the key stages of Umrah, starting with what it really means.

What is Umrah?

The word 'Umrah' comes from the Arabic root 'i'timar,' which means 'a visit,' but in Islamic terms, Umrah is much more profound. It refers to a pilgrimage to the Ka'bah in Makkah, performed with specific acts of devotion and worship. Unlike Hajj, which must be performed during Dhul-Hijjah, Umrah can be done at any time of year. This pilgrimage is an act of worship that allows us to come closer to Allah, to ask for forgiveness, and to renew our faith. Allah emphasizes the importance of pilgrimage in the Qur'an, saying, **"Complete the Hajj and Umrah for Allah"** (Qur'an 2:196). By undertaking Umrah, we are fulfilling a sunnah of the Prophet Muhammad (PBUH), who encouraged his followers to visit the Ka'bah and seek closeness to Allah.

The Core Steps of Umrah

Umrah consists of four main rituals: Ihram, Tawaf, Sa'ee, and Halq (or Taqsir). Each of these holds its own spiritual and symbolic significance. Here's a step-by-step guide to help you approach each stage mindfully and with a full heart.

Step 1: Entering Ihram

As you prepare to enter the sacred state of Ihram, it's essential to understand that this is not merely about changing clothes; it's about transforming your mindset and embodying a state of humility, equality, and purity. Ihram, meaning 'sacred' or 'forbidden,' is a state that signifies that you are undertaking this pilgrimage solely for Allah. You are preparing yourself, both outwardly and inwardly, to perform acts of worship in a state of complete submission.

Entering the State of Ihram: The Physical Preparation and Clothing

For men, Ihram consists of two unstitched white garments: one is wrapped around the waist, covering from the navel to below the knees, and the other is draped over the upper body. Importantly, men must remove any underwear, as the Ihram must remain simple and unstitched, symbolising humility and a stripping away of worldly identity. By removing stitched clothing, men become indistinguishable in status and wealth, standing as equals before Allah. The uniformity of Ihram clothing fosters a sense of unity and humility, erasing societal distinctions and reminding us of the equality of all believers in the eyes of Allah.

For women, Ihram involves wearing modest, loose-fitting attire that covers the entire body, excluding the face and hands. Unlike men, women are not restricted from wearing stitched clothing; they may wear any modest clothing as long as it adheres to the principles of covering and humility. While some women wear all-white attire to symbolise the purity of Ihram, others wear simple, loose-fitting garments in neutral colours. This is entirely permissible, as long as the clothing does not attract undue attention. For women, the focus is on covering and modesty rather than on the specific style of clothing. Women's Ihram allows them to maintain their modesty while fulfilling the requirements of the pilgrimage.

Ihram Prohibitions: Embracing Simplicity and Restraint

Entering Ihram imposes certain prohibitions on both men and women, serving as a reminder of the simplicity and restraint expected during this spiritual journey. The purpose of these restrictions is to help pilgrims detach from worldly concerns, focus on their worship, and cultivate a spirit of humility and purity. Here are the key prohibitions and guidelines to keep in mind:

1. **Personal Grooming:** Once in Ihram, both men and women are prohibited from trimming their hair, cutting their nails, or shaving any part of the body. This act of refraining from grooming serves as a reminder to let go of vanity and to embrace a state of natural simplicity in the presence of Allah.
2. **Scented Products**: Pilgrims must avoid all scented products, including perfumes, deodorants, and even scented soaps. Using unscented toiletries is essential, as the prohibition against fragrance is intended to help us shed superficial adornments and focus purely on worship.
3. **Hunting and Cutting Plants**: In Ihram, harming any living creature—even plants—is forbidden. Pilgrims should not hunt animals, cut plants, or damage any part of nature in the sacred boundaries. This rule instils respect for all of Allah's creations, reminding us of our duty to tread gently upon the earth.
4. **Physical Intimacy**: Sexual relations and any behaviour that may lead to arousal are strictly prohibited during Ihram. This rule emphasises the sanctity of the state of

Ihram, where the pilgrim's sole focus should be on devotion to Allah, free from worldly distractions.

5. **Covering the Head and Face**: For men, covering the head is prohibited while in Ihram. Men must leave their heads uncovered, symbolising openness and submission. However, men may cover their heads for protection against the sun if absolutely necessary, as long as they avoid structured hats or caps. For women, the face should remain uncovered. If a woman's niqab accidentally covers her face, she should lift it gently to avoid direct contact with the skin.
6. **Wearing Stitched or Structured Clothing (for Men)** In addition to removing underwear, men are also prohibited from wearing stitched or fitted garments, such as shirts, pants, or anything with seams that fit the body. They may not wear shoes that cover the ankles, so simple sandals or slip-ons are preferred.
7. **Shoes and Footwear**: Men are required to wear footwear that does not cover the ankle or top of the foot. Sandals are generally recommended, as they meet the requirements of Ihram while providing comfort. Women, however, may wear any closed shoes that are comfortable and modest, provided that they do not attract attention.

The Intention and Talbiyah: Declaring Your Purpose

As you approach the Meeqat, or boundary, where Ihram is officially entered, you are encouraged to make your niyyah (intention) in your heart with complete sincerity. You may also recite the niyyah aloud if you wish, though it is not required. With a heart filled with humility and devotion, make your intention, and then recite the Talbiyah aloud:

لَبَّيْكَ اللَّهُمَّ لَبَّيْكَ، لَبَّيْكَ لَا شَرِيكَ لَكَ لَبَّيْكَ، إِنَّ الْحَمْدَ وَالنِّعْمَةَ لَكَ وَالْمُلْكَ، لَا شَرِيكَ لَكَ

Labbayka Allahumma Labbayk. Labbayka la sharika laka Labbayk. Inna al-hamda wa an-ni'mata laka wa al-mulk. La sharika laka.

"Here I am, O Allah, here I am. Here I am, You have no partner. Here I am. Truly, all praise, favour, and sovereignty belong to You alone. You have no partner."

The Talbiyah is a declaration of submission and presence. As you recite these words, feel yourself answering Allah's call. This recitation should continue until you reach the Ka'bah, reinforcing your commitment and focus on this journey.

Each of these restrictions and acts within Ihram has a purpose, drawing you nearer to Allah with simplicity, sincerity, and humility. The Prophet Muhammad (PBUH) described the spirit of Ihram as an act of complete submission, where one's focus is shifted entirely towards worship. Embracing these limitations and the simplicity of Ihram helps us to detach from our worldly selves, entering a state of pure devotion as we approach the sacred precincts.

In this state of Ihram, you are reminded that the journey of Umrah is not just physical but deeply spiritual. You are shedding layers of material identity, submitting entirely to Allah, and embracing your place among all other believers as equal servants of the Divine.

Step 2: Tawaf

After entering Ihram, you will begin Tawaf, the act of circling the Ka'bah seven times in an anticlockwise direction. Tawaf is a powerful symbol of unity, as Muslims from every corner of the world come together, all circling the Ka'bah, with Allah at the centre of their hearts. Allah speaks of the Ka'bah as a gathering place, saying, **"And [mention] when We made the House a place of return for the people and a place of security"** (Qur'an 2:125).

How to Perform Tawaf: Start Tawaf facing the Black Stone (Hajr Al-Aswad), reciting, **"Bismillahi Allahu Akbar"** (In the name of Allah, Allah is the Greatest). Then, walk to your right so the Ka'bah remains on your left, making seven complete circles.

During Tawaf, focus on your connection to Allah. Avoid idle talk and use this time for supplications or personal duas. The Prophet (PBUH) recommended a particular dua between the Yamani Corner and the Black Stone, saying, **"Our Lord, give us good in this world and good in the Hereafter, and protect us from the punishment of the Fire"**(Qur'an 2:201). Let each step remind you that you are circling the heart of Islam, in unity with your fellow Muslims and in closeness to Allah.

Step 3: Sa'ee

Sa'ee is the act of walking seven times between the hills of Safa and Marwah, commemorating the journey of Hajar (AS), who ran between these hills in search of water for her son, Isma'il (AS). Allah, in His mercy, rewarded her perseverance, bringing forth the well of Zamzam, and honoured her devotion by making Sa'ee an essential part of both Hajj and Umrah. As you approach Safa, recite, **"Indeed, Safa and Marwah are among the symbols of Allah"** (Qur'an 2:158). Sa'ee embodies resilience and trust in Allah. Between the green markers, men are encouraged to walk briskly, imitating Hajar's urgency, while women proceed at their normal pace.

Step 4: Halq or Taqsir

The final ritual is Halq (shaving the head) or Taqsir (trimming the hair). For men, Halq is highly recommended, symbolising a fresh start and complete submission to Allah. Women trim a fingertip's length from the end of their hair, maintaining modesty and reverence.

With this step, you exit the state of Ihram, completing your Umrah. The Prophet (PBUH) described Umrah as an act that removes sins and brings forgiveness, saying, ***"One Umrah to another is an expiation for what is between them"*****(Bukhari).**

Acknowledgements

I would like to express my deepest gratitude to my family for their unwavering support throughout this journey. With profound humility, I extend my heartfelt gratitude to the many individuals who have shaped my journey, enriched my life, and given me memories to treasure forever. While this list could never be exhaustive, each name holds a special place, representing a meaningful chapter in my story.

Ustadh Sheikh Abdurrahman Madani, Mohamed Ali Harrath (CEO of Islam Channel), Ustadh Dr. Abdus Salam Azadi, Ustadh Dr. Abul Kalam Azad, Ustadh Mahmudul Hasan, Ustadh Sheikh Shady As Suleiman, Ustadh Sheikh Suleiman Ghani, Ustadh Yasrab Shah, Br. Golam Rasul, Moyeen Choudhury and the entire team at TV One, Engineer Abu Bakr Siddique (Chairman, Darus Salam, Dortmund, Germany), Md Ashique Hossain (President, DFIC Regina, Canada), Dr. Muhammad Asadullah, Associate Professor, University of Regina (Canada), Late Barrister Rizuan Rahman (Canada), Sadiqur Rahman (Chairman, Saskatoon Dawah Centre) Sheikh Mujahid Ali, Sheikh Shams ad Doha, Hafiz Mushfique Uddin, Salim Ahmad (Heart of Enfield Mosque) Syed Shaukat Ali (President – Al Khidmat UK), Hamza Ehtesham (Al Khidmat UK), The Board of Trustees Al Khidmat UK, Fazlul Alam Rubel & Mrs Afia Choudhury (Bluestone Travels), Hifzur Rahman (Labbayk Travels), Late Mizanur

Rahman Tipu (Bismillah Hajj & Umrah), Syed Imdadur Rahman (Madani Hajj Tours), Sami Sanaullah (Travelink), K M Abu Taher Chowdhury (Voice for Justice, London), Dr Hasanat Husain (Voice for Justice, London), Sheikh Shafi, Br. Ibrahim Jamali, Fawad Zafar, Br. Sabooh Uddin, Br. Arfan Ali, Imam Qasim, the entire team at Global Aid Trust, Yousaf Razzaq, Firdaus Mughal (Yasin), Sheikh Shah Mizanul Haque, Imtiaz Gul, Majid Rahman, Ashraf Moallem, Paul, and the entire Islam Channel team.

Each of you has played a role in shaping my journey and inspiring me to move forward with purpose and sincerity. May Allah (SWT) bless you abundantly for your contributions and companionship in this life and the Hereafter.